The College of Law

of England and Wales

CHANDOS
INFORMATION PROFESSIONAL SERIES

Series Editor: Ruth Rikowski
(email: Rikowskigr@aol.com)

Chandos' new series of books are aimed at the busy information professional. They have been specially commissioned to provide the reader with an authoritative view of current thinking. They are designed to provide easy-to-read and (most importantly) practical coverage of topics that are of interest to librarians and other information professionals. If you would like a full listing of current and forthcoming titles, please visit our web site **www.chandospublishing.com** or contact Hannah Grace-Williams on email info@chandospublishing.com or telephone number +44 (0) 1993 848726.

New authors: we are always pleased to receive ideas for new titles; if you would like to write a book for Chandos, please contact Dr Glyn Jones on email gjones@chandospublishing.com or telephone number +44 (0) 1993 848726.

Bulk orders: some organisations buy a number of copies of our books. If you are interested in doing this, we would be pleased to discuss a discount. Please contact Hannah Grace-Williams on email info@chandospublishing.com or telephone number +44 (0) 1993 848726.

Presentations for Librarians

A complete guide to creating effective, learner-centred presentations

LEE ANDREW HILYER

Chandos Publishing
Oxford · England

Chandos Publishing (Oxford) Limited
TBAC Business Centre
Avenue 4
Station Lane
Witney
Oxford OX28 4BN
UK
Tel: +44 (0) 1993 848726 Fax: +44 (0) 1865 884448
Email: info@chandospublishing.com
www.chandospublishing.com

First published in Great Britain in 2008

ISBN:
978 1 84334 303 5 (paperback)
978 1 84334 304 2 (hardback)
1 84334 303 7 (paperback)
1 84334 304 5 (hardback)

British Library Cataloguing-in-Publication Data.
A catalogue record for this book is available from the British Library.

Typeset by Avocet Typeset, Chilton, Aylesbury, Bucks.
Printed in the UK and USA.

In memory of Mrs Judy Ackerman, who opened my eyes
to the wonderful world of layout and typography

Contents

Preface   xi

List of figures and tables   xv

About the author   xix

PART 1 HUMAN LEARNING AND LEARNING FROM PRESENTATIONS

**1   How people learn: human cognitive architecture and the
     learning process   3**

Introduction   3

What is learning?   4

What is knowledge?   5

Our cognitive architecture   7

Schema construction   8

How is information processed?   10

Cognitive load theory   13

Summary   16

Notes   17

2   Learning from presentations: Part 1 – a bad experience   19

Introduction   19

Vignette   20

Analysis   24

Summary   29

3 Learning from presentations: Part 2 – a good experience   **31**

Introduction   31

Vignette   31

Analysis   36

Mayer's cognitive theory of multimedia learning   38

Mayer's multimedia design principles   39

What are the implications for presenters?   43

Summary   43

PART 2 CREATING A LEARNER-CENTRED PRESENTATION

4 Introduction to the presentation process model   **47**

Stage 1: Preparing for your presentation   49

Stage 2: Practise your presentation   49

Vignette   50

Stage 3: Present your presentation   50

Stage 4: Review your performance   51

Summary   52

5 Getting started   **53**

Getting organized   53

Logistical details   54

Assessing audience needs   55

Determining your goals   56

Conduct any necessary research   58

Summary   59

6 Writing your script and creating your storyboards   **61**

Writing your script   62

Storyboards   63

Summary   67

Note   67

Suggested further reading   68

7   Creating your slides   **69**

Slide layouts   70

Recommended sequence of slides   71

Using themes/slide designs   84

Using text in visuals   84

Using images and diagrams   89

Diagrams and statistical displays   92

Summary   97

Suggested further reading   97

8   Creating effective handouts   **99**

Handout formats   101

Other sources for handouts   106

When to use handouts   106

Encouraging useful note-taking   107

Summary   107

Suggested further reading   108

9   Integrating your script, slides and handouts through

practice and rehearsal   **109**

Vignette   109

Summary   112

10 Delivering a successful presentation   **115**

Before you leave the office ...   115

Disaster planning   118

Delivering your presentation   119

Slide show controls   124

Managing questions   125

Concluding your presentation   125

Summary   126

Suggested further reading   126

11 Evaluation for improvement   127

    Types of evaluation   127

    Assessing learning   128

    Summary   129

Appendices

A   Using Microsoft PowerPoint 2007   133

B   Using Apple Keynote Version 3   153

C   Using OpenOffice Impress Version 2.2   167

References   183

Index   *187*

Preface

Why I wrote this book

In 2004, I entered graduate school in the College of Education at the University of Houston. My intent was to obtain a second Master's degree in instructional technology to open the door to a possible career change. During my studies, I read an article by Steven Bell and John Shank entitled 'The blended librarian' (2004). The authors posit that the duties performed by academic librarians will need to expand beyond the traditional skill set of librarianship. Bell and Shank argue that academic librarians will need to become instructional designers and technology trouble-shooters as well in order to be of greatest service to their patrons. I also picked up a book by Dr Richard Mayer entitled *Multimedia Learning* (Mayer, 2001), which outlined guidelines on creating effective multimedia presentations backed by extensive experimental results. These two publications had such an impact on me that I shared them with many colleagues and classmates. Mayer's work especially influenced my approach to teaching presentation skills, switching from a focus on 'appearance' to a focus on the learning outcomes of a presentation.

Unfortunately, that focus on learning outcomes was

missing from most of the presentations I attended at conferences and workshops. As an audience member, I often had to endure endless series of text-laden slides, made worse by the presenter narrating them verbatim to me. When these presentations were over, I rarely remembered what they were about and often threw away the accompanying handouts because they made no sense without the speaker's narration. Since presentations are an integral part of the professional life of a librarian, I wondered why the quality of presentations was so abysmal. Why would we waste our time and resources attending presentations of little or no value?

As I neared graduation in 2006, I realized that what was needed was a book incorporating relevant learning theories and the best instructional design to address the problem of creating effective, learner-centred presentations. This is my humble attempt to bring that information to librarians everywhere, so that audiences can learn from presentations that are designed with guidelines based on the best evidence available about how we learn and process information.

How is the book organized?

This book is designed either to be read cover to cover or consulted as needed for inspiration or guidance. The content is organized into two parts: Part 1 is an exploration of human learning and learning from presentations while Part 2 provides guidelines and techniques for writing a script, creating visuals and handouts, and delivering a presentation effectively. You will not find an endless series of how-to steps; rather you will be given information that can be used no matter what type of presentation software you use. Appendices at the end of the book provide specific information on three of the most popular slide presentation software programs available: Microsoft PowerPoint 2007, Apple Keynote 3 and StarOffice/OpenOffice Impress.

What will you be able to do with this book?

It is my hope that you will be able to use the methods and recommendations in this book to improve your skills and provide an effective, learner-centred presentation where your audience actually enjoys the presentation and leaves having learned something new.

On the Web

This book is just one of many attempts to disseminate effective presentation skills across the profession. For additional resources, visit the companion blog and website:

Blog: *http://presentations4librarians.blogspot.com/*

Website: *http://www.hilyer.info/presentations/*

References

Bell, S.J. and Shank, J. (2004) 'The blended librarian', *C&RL News*, 65 (7): 372–5.

Mayer, R.E. (2001) *Multimedia Learning*. Cambridge and New York: Cambridge University Press.

List of figures and tables

Figures

1.1	Diagram for a schema for the topic of cognitive information processing theory	9
1.2	The cognitive information processing model	11
1.3	How sounds and spoken narration are processed in working memory	12
1.4	How visuals are processed in working memory	12
1.5	How displayed text (as on a PowerPoint slide) is processed in working memory	15
4.1	The presentation process model	48
6.1	A hand-drawn storyboard template	64
6.2	A storyboard template created using PowerPoint	64
6.3	A sample title slide storyboard	65
6.4	Some sample slide storyboards	66
7.1	A slide layout with placeholders for text and graphics	71
7.2(a)	Sample title slide layout	73
7.2(b)	Modified title slide layout	73
7.2(c)	Modified title slide layout using a photograph as background	74

7.3(a)	Sample agenda slide layout	75
7.3(b)	Sample agenda slide using photographs	75
7.4	Sample 'key points' slide	76
7.5(a)	Sample 'bumper' slide layout (modified agenda layout)	77
7.5(b)	Sample 'bumper' slide layout (title card layout)	78
7.6	Content slide layout using a sentence headline	79
7.7(a)	Clip art should be used in light-hearted and less serious presentations	80
7.7(b)	Use photographs whenever possible to enhance the visual impact of your presentation	81
7.8	AVOID text-filled slides	81
7.9	Sample 'ending' slide	83
7.10	The difference between serif and sans-serif fonts	86
7.11	Some serif and sans-serif font options	86
7.12(a)	Dark text placed on a light slide background	89
7.12(b)	Light text placed on a dark slide background	89
7.13	Slide using *text* to describe a cyclical process	92
7.14	Slide using a *diagram* to describe a cyclical process	93
7.15	Slide with timeline represented as text	93
7.16	Slide with timeline represented graphically	94
7.17	Sample chart	96
7.18	Sample chart edited to remove 'chartjunk'	96
8.1	A common format for presentation handouts	100
8.2	'Notes Pages' handout format	101
8.3	Handout created using the 'Create Handouts in Word' option in PowerPoint	102
8.4	Handout in four-page format (A3 or 11" × 17")	104
A.1	The PowerPoint 2007 program layout	135
A.2	Placeholders on a title slide layout	136

A.3	Pre-defined slide layouts	137
A.4	The **Insert** tab of the Ribbon	138
A.5	File and print options available by clicking the Office 'jewel'	139
A.6	Text boxes on a slide layout	140
A.7	The Font menu in the **Home** tab	141
A.8	The **Insert Picture** dialogue box	142
A.9	Frame options for your images	143
A.10	Clip art placed on a slide	144
A.11	Shapes and lines available from the drawing toolbar	145
A.12	'Prefab' slide theme applied to presentation	146
A.13	The Notes pane	147
A.14	'Notes Pages' view of presentation	148
A.15	Slide transition options	149
A.16	Slide show controls	149
B.1	The Keynote 3 opening screen	154
B.2	Placeholders on a title slide master	155
B.3	Pre-defined slide masters	156
B.4	Click the *Fonts* icon to access font formatting options	157
B.5	Insert a picture using the Media browser	158
B.6	The shapes toolbar and some shape examples	159
B.7	The themes palette	160
B.8	Notes pane	161
B.9	Slide transition options	162
B.10	Slide show settings	164
C.1	The Impress program layout (drawing view)	169
C.2	Placeholders on a title slide layout	170
C.3	Pre-defined slide layouts	171
C.4	Use the **Insert** menu to add new slide objects	172
C.5	Text boxes on a slide layout	173
C.6	Toolbar formatting options	174
C.7	The **Insert Graphics** dialogue box	175

C.8	Shapes and lines available from the drawing toolbar	176
C.9	Load slide designs when needed	177
C.10	The Notes View	178
C.11	Slide transition options	179
C.12	Slide show controls	180

Tables

5.1	Checklist – logistical details	54
7.1	Sequence of slides for a typical presentation	72

About the author

Lee Andrew Hilyer MLIS, MEd is Coordinator of Interlibrary Loan Services for the University of Houston Libraries. Prior to that, Mr Hilyer was Assistant Director for Photocopy/Interlibrary Loan Services at the Houston Academy of Medicine – Texas Medical Center Library, where he developed the curricula for both beginner and advanced presentation skills classes. He has published two books on inter-library loan and graduated with a Master's degree in Education in December 2006.

The author may be contacted via the publishers.

Part 1
Human Learning and Learning from Presentations

How people learn: human cognitive architecture and the learning process

Introduction

In order to design effective, learner-centred presentations, librarians need to have a basic knowledge of how people learn, both in general and, more specifically, from multimedia presentations. Understanding the systems involved in human cognition (how people think and learn) is necessary for creating presentations that not only engage the learner, but that also assist him or her to utilize their mental capabilities to process the information presented as effectively as possible. This chapter begins with a brief section outlining some general theories and assumptions about human learning and defining related vocabulary. Then we will discuss and examine some key assumptions about both working memory and long-term memory, two structures that together comprise our cognitive 'architecture'. Next we will discuss some theories about how information is processed in conscious, working memory and about how that same information is stored and later retrieved from long-term memory. We will conclude this chapter with a brief look at cognitive load theory, which describes the mental effort involved in information processing and storage.

What is learning?

In the literature of cognitive psychology (the branch of psychology concerned with human thinking and learning), learning is generally defined as a relatively permanent change in an individual's behaviour, performance or knowledge as a result of experience or interaction with the world (Driscoll, 2005: 9; Hamilton and Ghatala, 1994: 1, 9). For most instructional and presentation situations, we can generally define learning in terms of the *retention* and *transfer* of information. *Retention* is the ability to remember information and recall it when needed. Reciting a friend's memorized telephone number is an example of retention; you are recalling *retained* information (the friend's phone number) that you previously stored in your long-term memory. Other examples of retention include recalling from memory the details of the subject coverage of a particular database or stating the rules of using Boolean operators (AND, OR, NOT) in a search query. *Transfer* refers to your ability to apply retained information to new situations. A student who *applies* the rules of using Boolean operators and performs a successful search of a research database such as INSPEC is demonstrating transfer of information and skills from previous experience or instruction to a real-world situation.

What is knowledge?

What exactly are learners 'retaining' or 'transferring' to new situations? Facts (names of the parts of the body, colours in the visible spectrum, etc.), procedures (rules for using Boolean operators, the sequence of steps required to create and send an e-mail message, etc.) and other types of information are processed, stored and later retrieved when needed. We refer to this body of stored information collectively as *knowledge*. There are generally considered to be two types of knowledge: *episodic knowledge*, that is knowledge of events experienced in your own life (i.e. your 'memories'), and *semantic knowledge*, that is your knowledge about a subject. Semantic knowledge can be further subdivided into *declarative* and *procedural* knowledge (Hamilton and Ghatala, 1994).

Declarative knowledge can best be described as 'the facts'. Your library's mailing address, how the Library of Congress classification system is subdivided and the parts of a book can all be described as declarative knowledge. *Procedural* knowledge, on the other hand, is generally described as knowledge of *how to do something*. Composing and sending an e-mail message, for example, requires procedural knowledge of how to use an e-mail program, along with procedural knowledge of how to start a new e-mail message and type its contents, as well as how to ultimately address and send the message to the recipient.

Notice in our example above that the relationship between declarative and procedural knowledge and between retention and transfer is dynamic and interdependent; to perform even the simplest of tasks requires the utilization of both. To complete the task successfully, the writer must recall various pieces of information such as the recipient's e-mail address or the meanings of the icons and buttons used in the e-mail program (declarative knowledge). The writer must then combine that knowledge with the procedural and motor knowledge required to manipulate the mouse, type on the keyboard and complete the appropriate sequence of steps to send the message.

Likewise, the recipient must also combine declarative and procedural knowledge in working memory to receive, open, read and act on the information contained within the message. To comprehend the contents of the e-mail message requires skill in reading. Facility with reading depends upon the extensive storage and quick retrieval of declarative knowledge about the meanings of letters, words and sentences, along with automatic application of the procedural knowledge of how to interpret the syntax, grammar and organization of a text.

Experts usually complete a task, such as reading or composing an e-mail message, in less time than novices do. This speed difference is due to a tendency for the recall of knowledge and execution of procedures to become 'automated' over time. With repeated practice (known as rehearsal), knowledge can be accessed more quickly and with less mental effort. When a student is first learning to read, he concentrates on the pronunciation and meaning of each individual word and pays little attention to the overall meaning of the sentence. As word meanings and sentence structures are memorized and rehearsed by the learner, the process becomes more and more automated and the student's reading speed and comprehension both improve.

As a presenter, you will want to create a presentation that enables your audience members to retain the main points of your presentation and to able to recall and apply them in future situations. You may be attending your library association's annual meeting and giving a conference presentation on a successful program at your library. One of the main points of your presentation might describe an unforeseen problem you encountered while implementing the program. Several months later, an audience member embarking on a similar project at their library remembers what she learned from your presentation, applies that knowledge and manages to avoid the very problem you forewarned her about, thus saving herself and her library considerable time, effort and expense.

Our cognitive architecture

Now that we can define learning and describe the two types of semantic knowledge, we can explore how declarative and procedural knowledge is processed, stored in and retrieved from memory, and how that stored knowledge is organized and structured. Human memory is often represented as a binary system consisting of short-term or *working memory*, a temporary storage space where information is processed, and *long-term memory*, where a vast amount of information is stored for future retrieval (Baddeley, 1998; Sweller, 1999).

Working memory

Working memory is our mental 'workspace' where we process and manipulate both new information being received as well as information retrieved from long-term memory. It is generally assumed that human working memory is capable of consciously handling only a few elements of information at one time, and that these elements remain for only a few seconds without any kind of rehearsal or manipulation.[1] Previous research seemed to indicate that the number of elements that could be retained in working memory at any one time was seven, plus or minus two (7 ± 2), as reported by Miller (1956). Further research has led to a refinement of this estimate: Sweller (1999) suggests that for most instructional purposes, a range of 2–4 elements is more likely, depending on their inherent complexity and the amount of effort required by the learner to process them.

Long-term memory

Working memory storage is temporary: elements not attended to will quickly disappear to make room for new ones. In order to retain information and be able to use it later, it must be stored for future retrieval. Long-term memory, as its name implies, is the part of memory devoted to permanent, indefinite storage of knowledge. When asked to recite the names of the planets of the Solar System, or to demonstrate hitting a baseball, needed information (often a combination of declarative and procedural knowledge) is retrieved from long-term memory and placed into working memory for active processing. The capacity of long-term memory is thought to be unlimited, though some knowledge, such as your ability to speak another language, may become irretrievable (i.e. be forgotten over time), especially if the information was not deeply encoded when first processed or if the information is not recalled and processed regularly.

Schema construction

It is hypothesized that knowledge in long-term memory is organized in large conceptual hierarchies known as *schema* (see Figure 1.1). Schemas are constructed of multiple informational elements formed into networks of varying sizes and complexities, depending upon the nature of the information being stored.

Figure 1.1 Diagram of a schema for the topic of cognitive information processing theory

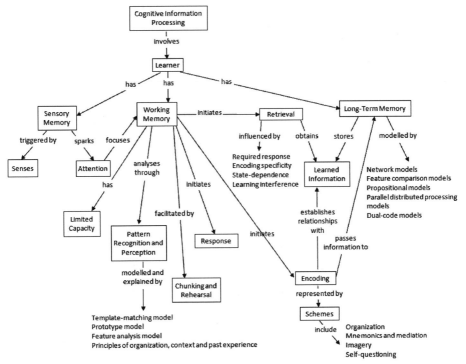

© Elena Northrup. Reprinted with permission.

Through learning, experience and practice, a person's schemas are constantly being created and modified. Smaller, related schemas will often combine to form larger and more detailed ones, whereas obsolete schemas will be neglected in favour of ones that are more relevant or replaced entirely by new ones. The formation of increasingly large and detailed 'super-structure' schemas helps to reduce the mental effort required to process information since a detailed schema can be manipulated as a single element in working memory, leaving additional processing capacity for new information.

Let us again consider our earlier example of sending and receiving an e-mail message. Veteran e-mail users usually do not complete the task of composing and sending an e-mail message through the activation of multiple schema; it is likely that these expert users maintain a highly detailed 'e-mail' schema in long-term memory and retrieve it when they need to send an e-mail message. With time and repeated practice, expert e-mail users combine what were previously separate schema (opening the program, composing the message, sending the message successfully, etc.) into a single, highly detailed schema. Because the super-structure schema represents only one element in working memory, the writer can use the additional available space in working memory to more efficiently compose the intellectual content of the message. Novice users, by contrast, must separately activate multiple schemas in order to complete the entire task, activating one schema for launching the program and opening a new message, another for composing the message, and yet another for addressing and sending the message.

How is information processed?

With a basic understanding of the human memory system, we can now turn our attention to the *process* of how we receive information, process it in working memory and encode it into our long-term memories for future retrieval. Cognitive information processing (CIP) theory provides a simplified theoretical model of how information is processed (see Figure 1.2). Based on the metaphor of how a computer processes information, CIP theory was adopted as a way to conceptualize human information processing, storage and retrieval.

| Figure 1.2 | The cognitive information processing model |

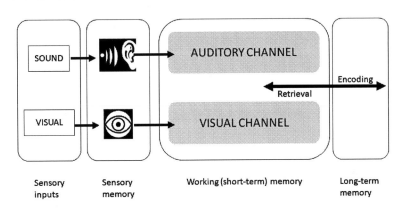

Source: Driscoll (2005: 74).

External auditory and visual stimuli (the presenter's spoken narration and her displayed PowerPoint slides, for example) are perceived by the senses and transferred to the learner's sensory memory. These inputs are quickly processed (within milliseconds) in sensory memory, then transmitted to working memory for possible attention and further processing. In order for learners to address this incoming input, they must *actively pay attention to it*; input that is not attended to will quickly fade from working memory.[2]

Once a learner focuses his attention on incoming input, that input is then normally processed via one of two channels in working memory,[3] depending upon the type of input received: sounds and spoken narration are processed in the *auditory channel* while images and displayed text are processed in the *visual channel* (see Figures 1.3–1.4) (Baddeley, 1998; Paivio, 1986).

Figure 1.3 How sounds and spoken narration are processed in working memory

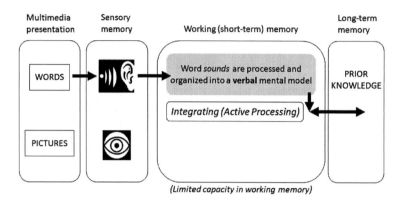

Figure 1.4 How visuals are processed in working memory

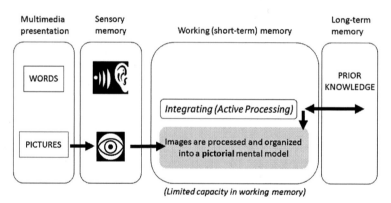

To process incoming information, the learner constructs a mental representation of the information to process it and possibly encode it in the form of a schema into long-term memory. This task is accomplished through the expenditure of mental effort on processing the information and constructing a mental representation of it, usually through *rehearsal* and/or *elaboration*.

Rehearsal means exactly that – a learner 'rehearses' the material through repeated exposure to or practice with it. Memorizing a friend's number by saying it repeatedly aloud is a simple example of rehearsal. *Elaboration*, by contrast, requires additional mental effort beyond simple rehearsal; the learner must manipulate the information in working memory. Sometimes elaboration includes the retrieval of previously stored information from long-term memory to assist in processing the new material. For example, someone who speaks French can retrieve and apply their existing knowledge of the grammar and syntax of the French language to help with learning the grammar and syntax of a related Romance language such as Spanish or Italian. Using new vocabulary words in sentences or applying algebraic formulas to solve a set of homework problems are just two examples of ways in which learners can elaborate upon material to be learned. Elaboration generally leads to better learning outcomes – as learners manipulate new information and combine it with existing prior knowledge, they often create richer and more abundant connections between the new information and prior knowledge and increase the chances of being able to recall and apply the information to new situations in the future.

Cognitive load theory

As mentioned earlier, processing information in working memory and encoding it into long-term memory requires mental effort from the learner, known as *cognitive load*. Current research indicates that the extent of cognitive load involved in a mental task is a decisive factor in a learner's success or failure in that task (Chandler and Sweller, 1991;

Sweller and Chandler, 1991, 1994; Sweller et al., 1990; Sweller et al., 1998; van Merrienboer et al., 2003). There are three types of cognitive load imposed by any mental task: *intrinsic* cognitive load, *extraneous* cognitive load and *germane* cognitive load. *Intrinsic* cognitive load is the inherent amount of mental effort required by the learning task and is determined, in part, by the goals (implicit or explicit) of the presentation (Clark et al., 2006). Memorizing a list of database names and their corresponding descriptions, for example, is a task with a small amount of intrinsic cognitive load. It may take some time and effort to memorize the list, but the actual mental effort required to memorize the list is minimal. By contrast, constructing a lengthy mathematical formula in a spreadsheet program is a more complex task and inherently carries a much higher level of intrinsic cognitive load.

Extraneous cognitive load refers to effort that is irrelevant to the learning task and should be minimized whenever possible. During a typical presentation, the presenter often presents content two ways: through his spoken words and through the PowerPoint slides (or other visuals) he chooses to display. If a displayed slide contains textual content similar to what the presenter is narrating, the level of extraneous cognitive load (and thus overall cognitive load) may increase. This is because textual information, while *initially* processed in the visual channel of working memory, is *diverted* to the auditory channel for final processing (Mayer, 2001; Mayer and Moreno, 2003) (see Figure 1.5).

Additionally, learners often expend unnecessary and irrelevant effort on mentally comparing and coordinating the written and spoken content of a presentation to discern the differences between the two, rather than focusing efforts on processing and understanding the presentation content itself.

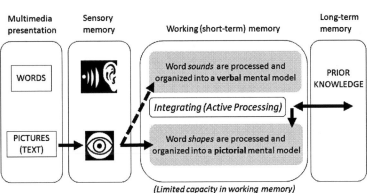

Figure 1.5 How displayed text (as on a PowerPoint slide) is processed in working memory

Unlike intrinsic cognitive load which you can do little about, or extraneous cognitive load which should be minimized whenever possible, *germane* cognitive load is important to successful and efficient learning. Clark et al. describe germane cognitive load as '... mental work imposed by instructional activities that benefit the instructional goal' (Clark et al., 2006: 11). Germane cognitive load can be increased any number of ways during a presentation or instructional session: by providing multiple examples for learners to elaborate upon, by interspersing lecture content with hands-on activities or by guided group discussion. If you were a librarian conducting a workshop on how to conduct a reference interview, you might provide your learners with a typical reference question from a public library, a school library and an academic library. You might also provide a variety of sample reference questions for learners to practise with, either as a hands-on activity or as structure for a group discussion. Providing multiple examples and utilizing hands-on practice activities does increase overall cognitive load, yet it is worthwhile as it can contribute to the successful completion of the learning process

Summary

Effective presenters design their presentations with an understanding and consideration of human learning, which we generally divide into retention (the ability to recall facts, dates, figures, etc.) and transfer (the ability to apply previously learned information to a new situation). Both declarative (facts) and procedural (how-to) knowledge are essential to the mastery of many mental and physical tasks. This knowledge is stored in long-term memory as intricate, hierarchical structures known as schema.

Schemas are adapted, expanded, subsumed or modified as new information is processed in working memory, the 'temporary workspace' where conscious mental processing takes place. Sensory inputs (speech, sounds and visuals) are processed through the two channels (auditory and visual) of working memory in preparation for possible encoding into long-term memory.

Unlike long-term memory, whose capacity is thought to be limitless, working memory can hold only about two to four elements at any one time. It is important for speakers to evaluate the potential cognitive load balance (intrinsic, extraneous and germane) of a presentation and its content. Presenters should deliver their presentations using methods and techniques that reduce extraneous cognitive load, increase germane cognitive load and support the creation of schemas. In the next two chapters, we will look more closely at two real-world presentation scenarios (one bad, one good) that will further examine how learning occurs (or does not occur) in a typical presentation situation.

Notes

1. This is known as the 'limited capacity' assumption about working memory. See Baddley (1998) and Chandler and Sweller (1991).

2. This is the 'active processing' assumption about working memory. See Mayer (2001), Paivio (1986), Sweller et al. (1990), Sweller et al. (1998), Wittrock (1989).

3. This is the 'dual-channel assumption' about the way working memory operates. See Mayer (2001), Paivio (1986).

Learning from presentations: Part 1 – a bad experience

Introduction

In Chapter 1, we discussed the basic structure of our cognitive architecture and reviewed the learning process. In this chapter, we will use that information to analyse the experience and learning outcomes of an audience member attending a typical conference presentation. As you read the short vignette below, consider your experiences both as a presenter and as an audience member: compare the speaker's performance with your own and compare the presentation situation described below to any recent ones you attended.

Consider also the issue of learning from the presentation. What does the *speaker* expect the audience to learn? What do *audience members* expect to learn? What new knowledge, if any, does the attendee obtain from the presentation? A detailed analysis follows the vignette to help you determine the answers to these questions.

Vignette

Listed in the conference programme:

Session Title: **How to Land the Job of Your Dreams**
Date: **20 November 2005**
Time: **11:30 – 12:30 (1 hour – including questions)**
Location: **Tiki Ballroom, Amazon Hotel**

Attention graduates! Need to know all of the tips and tricks to landing that first professional job? Fear not! Our speaker has over ten years' experience as the human resources director for the SuperGreat Library at Superb University. He will provide you with the information you need to create an attention-getting CV, craft a polished letter of application and sail through an interview with excellence!

Barbara has been looking forward to this presentation all day! She is about to graduate from university with a library science degree and is hard at work looking for a full-time position. She has been attending the conference mainly to look for employment, but has also managed to attend several presentations. She spotted the listing for this one last night in the conference programme while relaxing in her hotel room – she hoped it would be interesting and useful to her in her job search.

The introduction consisted of the chair of the programme committee detailing the two presenters' biographies through long lists of positions held and awards received. Barbara lost interest after about the first fifteen seconds (who wants to listen to a long list of degrees and published papers?) and had read about half of the handout she picked up when she heard the applause signalling that the introductions were over and the presentation itself was about to begin.

She refocused her attention on the speaker who walked to the podium. A laptop computer sat open and was connected to a large LCD projector, busily emanating the familiar Windows desktop – no one had as yet launched the speaker's slide presentation. Barbara could see a PowerPoint presentation file icon in the top-left corner of the screen. It had the presenter's name under it, so she assumed that was the file he would use. The speaker thanked the audience for coming and then double-clicked on his PowerPoint file to open it. The file opened in the program's default editing mode, and the presenter then treated the audience to twenty seconds of watching him search for the menu command to begin the slide show. Barbara's gaze began to drift back towards the handout in her lap.

Her attention was redirected toward the podium by the sudden blare of music from the loudspeakers – the presenter had decided to begin his presentation with a pop song. While the startled assistant in the back of the room scrambled up front to turn down the volume, the speaker began reintroducing himself. 'Haven't we already done this?' she thought to herself as she refocused her attention on the handout.

Several seconds later, the music stopped. Barbara looked up and realized that the speaker had moved on to his introduction. He spoke briefly about the current job market for library and information science and segued into a brief look at the latest salary survey results. Barbara was paying attention now, keen to get an idea of what kind of salary she could expect to receive. She pulled a pen from her purse and began to take notes in the margins of her handout.

What followed next was a succession of slides, each dense

with text from top to bottom, detailing the dos and don'ts of locating vacant positions, writing application letters, preparing a CV, interviewing and preparing for the first day on the job. Each time a new slide was displayed the speaker would turn his back to the audience and proceed to read each bullet point and sub-point in succession, occasionally turning back to the audience to pause for breath or to sip from his water bottle.

At first, Barbara tried to keep up. She would first listen to the speaker, then attend to the displayed slide. As she was reading the slide and listening to the speaker simultaneously, Barbara realized that she wasn't really listening to what the speaker had to say – she was listening for the difference between what the speaker said and what was displayed on the slide. Sadly, as the minutes ticked by, Barbara got tired of expending so much effort trying to comprehend both the spoken and displayed content and began to lose interest. 'The handout has all of the information anyway,' she thought to herself, 'I'll just follow along with that.'

With renewed focus on the speaker, Barbara sat poised and ready to take more notes. But trying to juggle all three information streams (speaker, slides and handout) wore her out and she completely gave up. 'I'll just read the handout later and get what I need,' she thought. Barbara slipped the handout into her tote bag, pulled out her exhibitors' map and spent the rest of the hour deciding which vendors she was going to visit when the presentation was over.

Barbara only paid attention to the speaker once more before she left the room. At the end of his presentation, the presenter boasted about how quickly he had created his slide show: 'I made it during the plane ride out here!' he cried, 'and I even managed to insert this MP3 file into the first slide on the taxi ride over here!' The audience chuckled politely, but Barbara did not. She was disappointed with the content of the presentation and felt that the last hour and a half had been a tremendous waste of her time. Meeting up with her colleagues in the exhibition hall later that day, Barbara could not recall the speaker's overall message, though she did manage to remember a few unrelated facts, mostly from the speaker's early discussion of salary levels.

Several weeks later, Barbara was busy preparing to start her job search and remembered that she still had the handout from the presentation. 'At least this may be helpful, even if his presentation wasn't,' she thought to herself. She pulled it out and sat back to read it.

Unfortunately, it wasn't much help. The speaker had chosen the default layout for handouts printed from PowerPoint: two columns, with the first being devoted to a thumbnail of the presented slide and lines for notes in the second. The speaker had used a dark background with light text and a gradient pattern in the background. At a reduced size, Barbara realized she could barely make out some of the smaller bullet points and could not read any of the URLs provided at all, because the transition from colour slide to black-and-white handout had converted the URL text colour from a light yellow to a grey that completely disappeared on the printed page. The notes she had made were not much help – notes made three weeks ago in the context of the presentation may have made sense to her then, but their meaning was now lost. She threw the handout into the recycling bin in disgust and decided she'd go and see what books the library had on the job application process.

Analysis

What a dreadful experience for Barbara! How many of you have also suffered through similarly awful presentations? Why do we commonly accept sub-par performances from our presenters or accept the status quo and continue to waste our time attending useless and boring presentations? Many presenters commonly prepare and deliver presentations that reflect more on the speaker's needs than on the needs of his audience. To identify some areas where our speaker's presentation and its delivery can be improved, let us now examine our vignette in more detail. As we do, keep in mind the information on human learning from Chapter 1 and think carefully about the speaker's assumptions about his content, his audience and learning in general.

We previously defined learning to be a relatively permanent change in behaviour, performance or knowledge. Many speakers use the limp verb 'inform' when articulating the overall goal of their presentation. To 'inform' someone about something implies a *passive* role for the recipient of the information. As mentioned earlier, learning is an active process that requires considerable mental effort from the learner. The speaker in our vignette committed the common mistake of focusing on the 'delivery' of information from speaker to audience rather than *communication* with the audience and assistance with the construction of knowledge. The implicit assumption in his presentation and its delivery was that the audience was responsible for processing this large amount of raw information. If the audience had listened to him, they would learn all they needed to know about conducting a successful job search from start to finish. If Barbara is any indication, however, the audience learned little from this gentleman's presentation.

With respect to human cognitive architecture, we can clearly see that the speaker's presentation posed some processing difficulties for Barbara. The vignette describes her difficulty in following the speaker's train of thought when he began working through a series of text-laden slides:

As she was reading the slide and listening to the speaker simultaneously, Barbara realized that she wasn't really listening to what the speaker had to say – she was listening for the difference between what the speaker said and what was displayed on the slide. Sadly, as the minutes ticked by, Barbara got tired of expending so much effort trying to comprehend both the spoken and displayed content and began to lose interest.

Audience members in a presentation are at a distinct learning disadvantage in that the content is presented in a linear, sequential fashion with little chance to 'rewind' and review past content. Contrast the activity of attending to a presentation with reading a journal article. The reader can read and re-read passages as many times as necessary in order to comprehend the information. Audience members have no such luxury – they are expected to efficiently process a 30- or 60-minute stream of simultaneously spoken and displayed information. When speakers fail to take into account the limitations of human cognitive architecture when presenting, they begin to set up a series of roadblocks for their audience members to overcome simply to comprehend the content.

One of the most common roadblocks created by presenters is an unintentional increase in the amount of extraneous cognitive load and therefore the increased possibility of cognitive *overload* (see section on 'cognitive load theory' in Chapter 1). Every learning situation contains the three types of cognitive load: intrinsic, extraneous and germane, all present in varying quantities. In our vignette, the main activity (listening to a speaker and watching some slides) exerted only a small amount of intrinsic cognitive load. However, the speaker's combination of spoken narration and text-filled slides to present his content increased the amount of extraneous cognitive load:

> The presentation of printed text in multimedia messages [such as a presentation slide] tends to create an information processing challenge for the dual-channel system ... when verbal material must enter through the visual channel, the words must take a complex route through [working memory] and must also compete for attention with the [visual material already being processed by the learner]. (Mayer, 2001: 61; see also Figure 1.5)

When Barbara attempted to compensate by taking notes, she added an additional information stream, which further increased her overall cognitive load. Small wonder she decided to give up completely and consult the handout later. Additionally, the speaker failed to explicitly describe what would be covered in the presentation or to provide any structure to the presentation content. Like Barbara, many audience members would have experienced cognitive overload and simply stopped paying attention to the speaker.

What was the amount of germane cognitive load in our vignette? Did our speaker use any techniques, methods or activities to increase the amount (remember that increased germane cognitive load is often beneficial to successful learning outcomes)? Were audience members encouraged to actively process the presented content, or was the speaker content to deliver his message to a passive audience? Good presenters employ techniques and direct activities that encourage learners to elaborate upon presented material and actively process it for understanding and further use. These types of activities often increase the germane cognitive load of the overall presentation but, if managed properly, ultimately benefit the learner.

In summary, our speaker presented the all-too-common 'data dump' of information to the audience with little structure and no cognitive guidance on how to organize it. Audience members had to waste limited cognitive resources on organizing and structuring the content, thus reducing the amount of resources available to actually process the presentation content. Working more from extensive bulleted lists rather than a thoughtful treatment of three to five important content points, the speaker used a plethora of text-laden slides to cover a laundry list of topics that left his audience more bored and confused than excited about their future job prospects.

Did learning occur?

Let us first investigate this question from the speaker's perspective. When questioned over lunch later in the day he stated that he had given his audience a 'comprehensive treatment' of many job search issues that will help them land their dream jobs. The speaker knew that he had 'deluged them with information', but was confident they had learned what to do and what not to do during a job search. He added that he had given the audience a handout of his slides – he was sure they would be useful to attendees. He implied (half seriously) that if the audience just followed his suggestions then they would all have jobs within a week.

Let us now try and answer the question from Barbara's perspective. Does she feel like she learned anything? Barbara certainly remembers attending the presentation, what the speaker looked like, how poor the lighting was and that the room itself smelled of burnt coffee. In short, Barbara has abundant episodic knowledge (memories) of the event itself. What about semantic knowledge, though? Did Barbara acquire any new knowledge or skills that she could use immediately in her job search? According to Barbara, she gained '... very little, if any' new knowledge from the speaker's presentation. The speaker overwhelmed her with information presented three ways: in verbal form, as on-screen text and in a paper handout. Without any explicit cognitive guidance for how to process the presentation, the amount of information presented actually induced cognitive overload, in Barbara's mind and in the minds of many of the other audience members. When faced with cognitive overload, Barbara, like most learners, simply 'shut down' and diverted her attention elsewhere: 'Barbara slipped the handout into her tote bag, pulled out her exhibitors' map and spent the rest of the hour deciding which vendors she was going to visit when the presentation was over.'

Not even the handout managed to be helpful or to promote Barbara's learning. Without the speaker's verbal narration, some of the slides on the handout made no sense, and the text on some of the slide thumbnail images was unreadable. She feared misinterpreting the information and making a ghastly mistake on her CV or on one of her job application letters.

Summary

To increase the possibility of positive learning outcomes, presenters must consider the limitations of human cognitive architecture and structure their material in ways that assist learners to actively process the presented information. In our vignette, the speaker clearly disregarded these limitations and the result was a poor learning outcome for the audience. In the following chapter, we will accompany Barbara to another presentation on career planning, this time with a much more successful outcome.

3

Learning from presentations: Part 2 – a good experience

Introduction

Poor Barbara. Graduation day is fast approaching and she still needs to learn more about successfully conducting her job search. One of her colleagues stopped her in the lounge to tell her about another career-planning seminar being held later in the week at another local university library. She is desperate for information, so she plans to attend, hoping that this presentation will be better than the last.

Vignette

Barbara arrives at the seminar, which is being held in a lovely, second-floor classroom with floor-to-ceiling windows, comfortable chairs and a pleasant temperature (at the presentation last month, the windowless room was extremely stuffy). She is a few minutes early, but she notices that the presenter has already started the PowerPoint slide show. Displayed on the screen is the title of the show ('Plant the Seeds of Job Search Success!'), the presenter's name and a countdown clock which is marking the time until the presentation begins. The slide's background colour is a pleasant green, with the text set in white for good contrast. Also on the slide is a lovely photograph of a tree, which Barbara realizes is reinforcing the idea behind the title of the presentation. Rather than nervously fumbling with equipment or shuffling note cards, the presenter is engaged in conversation with several members of the audience down in front. She looks around for handouts, but does not see anything near the door. She takes a seat near the middle of the room, settles in and waits for the presentation to begin (which, according to the countdown timer, is in 4 minutes and 33 seconds).

Barbara can hear the presenter asking questions and becoming better acquainted with the audience, even before the presentation has begun! 'I've never seen a presenter do that before,' she thought to herself. When the countdown timer reached zero, a series of three soft chimes played. The speaker completed his conversations, stepped back to the podium, turned on his microphone and began the presentation.

'Good afternoon, everyone and welcome! I know that you are eager to begin planting your own "Seeds of Job Search Success" so let us get started right away! I have already talked with many of you in the audience, asking you what YOU want to leave with when our time is up today. I'm comforted to have heard many of you listing topics that I have prepared for today and I assure you that there will be plenty of time for questions and opportunities for discussion about today's material.' During this time, Barbara barely noticed that the speaker had picked up a small remote and had moved out from behind the podium. She was already focused on the presenter and ready to learn.

The speaker's next slide was entitled 'Agenda' and it listed four areas that the speaker intended to cover:

1. *Locating job ads*

2. *Writing CVs and cover letters*

3. *Interviewing*

4. *Starting your new job.*

The speaker spoke briefly (1–2 sentences) on each topic, emphasizing that the detail would be coming later. The next slide instructed the audience to focus on three key overall points:

1. *Finding the right job for your skills*

2. *The importance of proofreading and external review*

3. *Practise, practise, practise!*

He signalled to the audience that they could organize their thinking around these three key points and that he would be sure to tie content back to those main points. He picked up a folder from the table in front of him and displayed it to the audience: 'You can take notes if you want, if that is what helps you learn best, or you can listen. The folder I have prepared for you contains a written summary of what we will be covering today, along with some sample CVs, cover letters and a list of typical interview questions for practice. There will also be opportunities for group discussion, because many of you have completed this process before and have much to contribute.'

The presenter then moved on to each of his four listed topics, one by one. Barbara noticed that each time the presenter moved to another section, a slide with nothing but the topic title was displayed, serving as a visual indicator of the upcoming material. The presenter's slides overall had a spare and clean layout; sometimes he used a funny photo to make a point, other times he displayed diagrams to illustrate a concept, and sometimes he just put one or two sentences on the slides. Barbara noticed none of the slides used bullet points, unlike the previous presentation she attended, where they had been present in abundance.

During each section, the presenter also opened the floor up for discussion and sharing from audience members. He was careful to encourage everyone to contribute, and he personalized the presentation by mentioning some of the audience members whose names/situations he had learned of earlier. Each time he moved to the discussion phase, he would press a button on his remote to black out the screen and he would move closer to the audience to listen to the discussion better. Best of all, before moving to another section, the speaker displayed a slide with three large columns on it, with each column heading corresponding to the speaker's suggested three takeaway points. As they moved through the sections of the presentation, the speaker added section information to each of these columns, with the result being that at the end of the presentation, he was able to present a completed 'chart' of the three takeaway points and some supporting information for each of them.

During the section on CVs and application letters, the speaker distributed several samples to the audience and allowed a few minutes for the audience to review them silently. The slide displayed on the screen indicated what section they were in, what activity they were doing and a countdown clock to keep the time limit. As earlier, a series of soft chimes were used to mark the end of the silent review period. This brought the audience back to attention on the presenter, who then led a discussion about the strengths and weaknesses of the sample CVs and application letters.

The speaker next used short video clips to illustrate common pitfalls in interviewing and guided the audience through some strategies for handling tough questions. The video clips were not full-blown productions; in some of them, the speaker himself played the part of an interviewee, but Barbara thought they were an engaging and useful way to illustrate the concepts without having to participate in any role-playing, which she disliked.

Throughout the presentation, Barbara remained engaged and attentive. She found the presenter's use of images to be helpful to her in making connections among the material, and she especially enjoyed the video clips on interviewing. The speaker clearly signalled to the audience (sometimes verbally, sometimes visually) when he was presenting key supporting information related to one of the three key takeaway points. The speaker had recommended that if the audience was going to take notes that they attempt to organize them in their notebook via the three-point structure. That way, he said, they would have an overall organizational structure to guide their learning and knowledge construction.

At the end of the presentation, the speaker reviewed the material covered, not by going over the four sections again, but by showing the completed, three-column diagram that corresponded with his three key points, a copy of which was included in each packet of information. He concluded his final review with a few real-life anecdotes, thanked his audience for their attention and advanced to the next slide in his deck which simply read 'Questions?'

Barbara was amazed that an hour had gone by! At no time during this presentation did she feel overwhelmed with content. The speaker's reliance on images and diagrams helped to reinforce his spoken content and she knew that when she left and began her job search in earnest that the presenter's three key takeaway points would remain with her as guiding principles. He spoke at a dynamic but measured pace, pausing often so note-takers could catch up with him. He asked for clarification from the audience at appropriate intervals to be sure they comprehended his content. She had planned to leave after the presentation and before the question-and-answer period, but the discussion was so lively that she stayed until the very end, after the speaker had been leading a discussion and answering questions for nearly 45 minutes! On the way home, Barbara phoned a fellow student to let her know how fantastic the presentation was and what she had learned. She had not had a chance to review the handout folder yet, but she knew it would be good.

As promised, the folder contained a one-page written summary of what the speaker had covered, the three-column diagram of key takeaway points and supporting text, additional sample CVs and cover letters, and a bonus list of employment and other career websites. Several weeks later when Barbara began to apply for open positions in earnest, she found that she often referred back to the folder for guidance on constructing her cover letters and for searching jobsites. She shared the folder with many of her classmates who were not able to attend and it became dog-eared from use during the four months it took for her to secure a professional position.

Analysis

It is clear from the vignette that this speaker, unlike our previous one, knows how to design and deliver a learner-centred presentation. His slides and his spoken content were delivered in a fashion consistent with the limitations of our cognitive architecture and he created the conditions for learners to connect and integrate the verbal information with the visual information. This speaker's 'three key points' structure gave the audience a cognitive 'scaffold' which they could use to construct their own schema for organizing and processing the information from the presentation. The speaker knew that simply doing a 'data dump' would not be helpful for already nervous, soon-to-be graduates, so he focused on a few key points and presented supporting evidence and additional detail for each of those three points. He knew that the audience would not remember every single thing he said, but if they had time to elaborate on the material presented and if he explicitly structured his content for the audience, then there would be a much greater chance that the audience would retain the main points and use them (and related details) later in their own personal situations.

He increased the amount of germane cognitive load by having the audience elaborate on the material in multiple ways. In the initial section of the presentation, he led a discussion on the best and worst career websites and the audience collaboratively created some quick guidelines for evaluating them. During the second section, he distributed samples of cover letters and CVs and allowed the audience several minutes to review and begin to evaluate them critically. The video clips used in the section on interviewing were followed by group discussions to elaborate further on the information presented. Throughout the presentation, the speaker repeatedly encouraged his audience to connect his presentation content with their own prior knowledge and experiences.

The speaker's folder of handouts was designed to *supplement* the presentation, not to be a substitute for it. Rather than simply print his slides as a handout, which is common practice, he took the time and trouble to prepare supplementary material that the audience would (he hoped) make use of in the future.

Did learning occur?

Quite simply, yes. Barbara was engaged and attentive throughout the presentation. The speaker helped her to organize her learning by providing an explicit, three-point structure she could use to organize the details. She had time and opportunity during the presentation to elaborate on the information given and the *careful combination of spoken and visual content* enabled her to form robust mental models. She left with a folder full of supplementary material she could use to refresh her memory later. She was so happy with the outcome that she enthusiastically shared the folder with her classmates.

The speaker knew that if he worked within the limits of human cognitive architecture, encouraged active processing of the material and made every attempt to minimize extraneous cognitive load his learners would stand a better chance of acquiring the knowledge they needed to more efficiently and more successfully conduct a job search. Having studied human learning in graduate school and having trained in multimedia creation, the speaker used research-based design principles to design and deliver a learner-centred presentation. Audience members were able to actively process the information presented, retain it and use it in later situations as they applied for open professional positions.

Mayer's cognitive theory of multimedia learning

Richard Mayer, professor of educational psychology at the University of California – Santa Barbara, has spent nearly twenty years exploring multimedia learning, and has developed a 'cognitive theory of multimedia learning' which describes the processes involved in meaningful learning from multimedia presentations (Mayer, 2001; Mayer and Moreno, 2003). Simply stated, the theory posits that people learn better from words and pictures than from words alone. Our vignette above describes a presentation prepared and delivered by someone familiar with, and confident in, the hypotheses of Mayer's theory.

Through extensive experimental research, Mayer's theory has defined seven principles of multimedia design. These have yielded practical guidelines that can be applied to the creation and delivery of presentations to encourage meaningful and active processing, decrease extraneous cognitive load and increase the potential for a successful learning outcome.

Mayer's multimedia design principles

1. *Multimedia*. People learn better from words and pictures than from words alone.

   The fundamental idea behind using slides or other visuals during a presentation.

2. *Spatial contiguity*. People learn better when words and pictures are presented near to each other.

   In diagrams, graphics and text should be near each other to reduce the amount of 'visual search' required by learners. This has been tested using textbooks and is applicable both to slides and to handouts.

3. *Temporal contiguity*. People learn better when words and pictures are presented simultaneously.

   The fundamental way a presentation is delivered – the presenter speaks while displaying relevant slides.

4. *Coherence*. People learn better when extraneous material is excluded from the presentation.

Pare your presentation content down and remove material irrelevant to the main points.

5. *Modality*. People learn better with spoken words and animation than with animation plus on-screen text.

Using animation (or detailed visuals) with on-screen text creates a potential cognitive overload in the visual channel. By offloading some of that content from on-screen text to spoken narration, load in the visual channel is reduced.

6. *Redundancy*. People learn better when animation and narration are used rather than when animation, narration and on-screen text is used.

As discussed in Chapter 1, displayed text is processed both in the visual channel and in the auditory channel. Presenters should be sure not to overload either channel in working memory, which can occur when presenters deliver redundant content through one or more methods (spoken, visual, displayed text).

7. *Individual differences*. 'Design effects are stronger for low-knowledge learners than for high-knowledge learners and for high-spatial learners rather than for low-spatial learners' (Mayer, 2001: 184).

While not a panacea for all presentation situations, principles 1–6 outlined above can help increase the learning effectiveness of a presentation. However, Mayer and his colleagues have discovered that high-knowledge learners (experts) do not see the same improvement in retention and transfer as low-knowledge learners (novices) do. The same is true for high-spatial learners (learners who can easily create and manipulate mental visual images) versus low-spatial learners (those who have more difficulty generating them).

(Mayer, 2001)

Librarians can utilize these design principles when creating and delivering their presentations to increase the possibility that learning will occur. The techniques, methods and recommendations presented in Part 2 are based upon the above principles.

What is a multimedia presentation?

Mayer defines a multimedia presentation as presenting material that is processed via the visual and auditory channels (Mayer, 2001: 7). Multimedia can be as simple as a professor giving a spoken lecture and using a chalkboard or something as complex as an elaborate production with music, video and dazzling special effects. A presentation with a speaker and PowerPoint slides is a multimedia presentation delivering information via two formats: (1) the spoken content of the presenter (processed in the auditory channel); and (2) the displayed slides (processed in the visual channel). While much of Mayer's research has focused on learning from computer-based animations of cause-and-effect explanations (how lighting works, how pumps work, etc.) such as those found in a multimedia encyclopaedia, the relevant principles are applicable to a wide range of common multimedia presentation situations faced by librarians.

How do we learn from multimedia presentations?

Mayer outlines five cognitive processes that a learner must engage in when learning from multimedia (Mayer, 2001: 54):

1. **Selecting** relevant *words* (verbal information) for further processing.

2. **Selecting** relevant *images* (visual information) for further processing.

3. **Organizing** selected *words* into a verbal mental model.

4. **Organizing** selected *images* into a visual mental model.

5. **Integrating** verbal and visual mental models.

Meaningful and active processing of information helps the learner to successfully integrate the verbal and visual mental models, resulting in high retention of the knowledge and high transfer of that knowledge to new situations (Mayer, 2001: 17).

Learners engage in these five processes during a multimedia presentation. In our vignette above, Barbara listened to the speaker's spoken narration and selected relevant verbal information for further processing. Simultaneously, she looked at the speaker's slides and selected particular images (or parts of diagrams) for additional processing. She then organized both the verbal information and the visual information into separate verbal and visual mental models, integrated them together and connected aspects of the new models to her own prior knowledge (when it was available). The creation of mental models is also known as schema construction, which was briefly described in Chapter 2. New schemas are formed for new information, and existing schemas are often modified when new, related knowledge is constructed in long-term memory.

What are the implications for presenters?

It is the presenter's responsibility (this means YOU) to create and deliver a presentation that not only presents information to learners, but also provides guidance for *how* to process that information, that is, guidance '... for determining what to pay attention to, how to mentally organize it and how to relate it to prior knowledge' (Mayer, 2001: 15). This is exemplified in our above vignette: our speaker first described the overall structure of the content of his presentation and then proceeded to organize his content according to that structure, giving learners in the audience explicit guidance for processing the presented material. His spoken text and accompanying visuals were crafted with consideration for the limitations of human working memory, and he used verbal and visual cues to signal the audience to attend to certain key pieces of information during the presentation. His discussions and activities guided the audience to elaborate on the new content and to relate the new content to existing prior knowledge.

Summary

In the last chapter, we endured an awful presentation with our friend Barbara. This chapter described a more pleasant and, more importantly, a more effective, learner-centred presentation experience. The dramatic difference between the two vignettes can be traced to the second speaker's understanding of the limitations of working memory, of meaningful learning and of how cognitive load affects it. With some relatively simple changes to the way you prepare and deliver presentations, you can drastically improve the odds that your presentation will be a success, that your audience will enjoy themselves and that they will leave the auditorium having learned something new. To get you started, Chapter 4 will describe a comprehensive presentation design process that incorporates all of the relevant assumptions about our cognitive architecture and learning theories discussed so far. Its goal will be to provide you with a comprehensive model of creating and delivering learner-centred presentations.

Part 2
Creating a Learner-Centred Presentation

Introduction to the presentation process model

All presenters utilize some process (either explicit or implicit) when they plan for and deliver their presentations. The process detailed below is a general framework based on the theories and assumptions outlined in Part 1 that I use to create my own presentations. Intended as explicit guidance for novice presenters and as a refresher for those more experienced, this chapter provides a model of the process, with subsequent chapters describing in more detail particular techniques and methods you can use. Depending on your knowledge, skill level and experience you can modify this process to suit your own personal situation and presentation requirements.

This process model describes an attempt at an *instructional design theory* for effective presentations. Unlike many theories which are descriptive, an instructional design theory is prescriptive, recommending particular methods of instruction and information design for a particular content area and a particular audience (see Reigeluth, 1999). Instructional design theories develop from a number of areas: the instructor's own experience, evidence in the research literature supporting one method or another, audience characteristics, the nature of the content covered, the desired learning outcomes and even other theories (both learning and instructional design theories). For example, many of the techniques described in subsequent chapters are derived from the research results of experiments conducted to test aspects of the theories of multimedia learning and cognitive load.

There are four stages to the presentation process (see Figure 4.1):

1. Prepare

2. Practise

3. Present

4. Review

Figure 4.1 The presentation process model

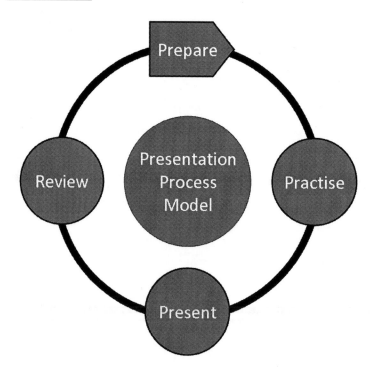

Stage 1: Preparing for your presentation

Once you accept an invitation to speak or your conference proposal is accepted, you begin *preparing* for your presentation. This involves not only writing your speech and creating your slides, but also identifying your goals, analysing your audience and gathering the logistical details of when, where and how you will present. The foundation of a successful presentation is proper preparation.

Stage 2: Practise your presentation

Next, you must *practise* delivering your presentation. I cannot stress enough how important practice is to a smooth and professional presentation. Practising helps nervous speakers remain calm and helps veteran speakers to rigorously prune the content of their presentation until only the most effective and relevant information remains.

It is important to begin planning early to give yourself ample time to practise, either alone or with someone else, or by videotaping or audio taping yourself. Recently, I decided to completely revise a standard, two-hour presentation class I have been teaching for several years. It was time to update the class, especially to incorporate some more discussion and activities regarding Mayer's theory of multimedia learning and how it can be applied to presentations. After spending nearly 18 hours resequencing the content and restructuring the activities, I decided to go and practise in an available training classroom.

Vignette

I had estimated the times required for each of the various modules of the presentation but found that I was woefully inaccurate with my initial predictions. Some sections took only half the expected time to cover, but two others required an additional 15 minutes each. My practice session (including time-outs to take notes) took four hours. Immediately, it was apparent to me that I would not be able to cover all of the material I wanted to share in two hours, so I had to further shift material from my slides to either my script (my spoken words) or my handouts.

A subsequent practice session using the further refined presentation ended up at just under two hours. Had I been overconfident of my abilities and my preparations, in a live class I would have only covered half of my planned material and would not have been able to provide my audience with a coherent presentation of information. Certainly I was disappointed to have to cut some material (there is so much to say on effective presentations), but I wanted to focus on the essential information, those 3–5 key points about presentations that I wanted the audience to walk away wanting to incorporate into their own presentations. Some of the material I originally included was less relevant to those main points and was moved to the handout or discussed during the subsequent question and answer period.

Stage 3: Present your presentation

The third component of the presentation process is the *delivery* of the presentation itself. The word 'delivery' is something of a misnomer, as what you really want to do is to establish a 'conversation' with the audience. Delivering a presentation is not just a matter of saying the words and clicking the mouse; it requires engaging the audience in a conversation on a topic you feel strongly about and utilizing the most effective instructional methods available to communicate your message. Besides ample practice, there are many techniques and methods you can employ as a speaker to improve your delivery and engage your audience. Chapter 10 will discuss presentation delivery in more extensive detail.

Stage 4: Review your performance

The fourth component of the process is *reviewing* your performance, the effectiveness of your presentation and your audience's learning outcomes. Once we finish a presentation, we often breathe a sigh of relief and never give another thought to it again. However, if you want to continuously improve your presentation skills, then it is imperative that you set aside time for real reflection, assessment and evaluation of your presentation and its outcomes. This can be accomplished in many ways: through evaluation survey forms completed by your audience, through personal reflection on your own performance or through review of a video or audio recording of your performance. Chapter 11 provides guidance on gathering and evaluating feedback, including some recommended sources for locating useful evaluation questions.

Summary

This chapter introduced you to a model of the presentation process by briefly describing each of its four stages (Prepare – Practise – Present – Review). In the following chapters, we will explore each stage of the process in detail, covering your initial preparations (Chapter 5), writing a great script and creating effective slides (Chapters 6–7). Crafting handouts your audience will want to keep is the subject of Chapter 8 while integrating the three (script, slides and handouts) into a coherent whole is described in Chapter 9. We will also look at the rehearsal process as an editing tool to help you refine your content and solidify your message (Chapter 10). Finally, we will discuss the importance of evaluation of your performance (Chapter 11) to gather data you can use to identify ways to improve.

5

Getting started

Your first steps toward a successful presentation involve getting organized for the work ahead, gathering the logistical details (where, when, what conference, travel details, etc.), and assessing your audience's needs and wants. Your next step is to determine what content you can provide to meet those needs, and how best to communicate that content to the audience.

Getting organized

Depending on the requirements to be met, a lengthy presentation might involve extensive research and collection of media resources, which can easily become more complicated to manage. Set aside a folder on the desktop of your computer and designate a paper folder to hold your drafts, notes and other documents related to the presentation. When storing your digital files, save them all into this folder to keep everything together in one place. For PowerPoint users, this also ensures that all of the links between the presentation file and any large media files (movie files, mp3 files and CD tracks) remain intact. PowerPoint embeds images into a presentation file, but only *links* to large files; keeping all of your media and PowerPoint files in one place helps prevent any broken links. In your paper folder, keep master copies of your handouts, a copy of your script and any other documents you might need to refer to as you prepare your presentation.

Logistical details

As part of your initial preparations, don't forget about the obvious details (room location, date, time, equipment available, etc.) and the not-so-obvious ones: is your time slot right after lunch? If so, plan on some energizing activities to engage your sleepy audience. Table 5.1 provides a checklist of items to consider as you gather your logistical details.

Table 5.1   Checklist – logistical details

- Title (tentative – just to give you something to work with initially)
- Date and time of presentation
- Venue/location
- For (who's the audience?)
- Format of the presentation (keynote, panel, conference, workshop, instruction)
- Length of presentation (is a Q&A period included or separate?)
- Why are you giving the presentation (supporting your research proposal, professional development, hired speaker)?
- What methods will you use (speech, slides, other media, objects, activities)?
- What equipment needs do you have? Who will supply these?

Assessing audience needs

To understand your audience's needs it is important to first be able to clearly describe your audience for this presentation. Are you presenting to peers, students or community leaders? What are they like? Can you describe them and what they might do with your information (how will it help them)? While you may not know your audience beforehand, you can probably at least speculate on who might be interested in the content of your presentation. Of course, sometimes your lecture hall or classroom will be filled with a wide variety of interested attendees. While you cannot meet the needs of every person in the audience, you should do your best to ensure your content is appealing and relevant to as many sectors of your audience as is possible and appropriate for your situation.

What is their level of prior knowledge?

Another dimension to consider is your audience's experience with your content (their prior knowledge). If you are presenting to a group of experts, you will need to concentrate on the aspects of your content or research that are most relevant to them. Novices to your content, by contrast, may need more introductory material.

Here are some sample questions you might want to use with your own audience analysis:

1. Who will be in the audience (students, faculty, colleagues, community leaders, etc.)?

   A presentation for librarians will be different from a presentation for community leaders.

2. What is their level of prior knowledge with the subject of your presentation?

A presentation delivered to experts on a subject, for example, will be vastly different one given to novices in a subject.

3. Why is the audience attending your presentation? What do they want to know?

You have some idea why your audience is attending, but are you really thinking about what they might want to know, or are you just concerned with what you think they should know?

Spend a few minutes jotting down some answers to the above questions about your audience; describing your audience and anticipating their needs helps you delineate the depth and breadth of the content you will present.

Determining your goals

Analysing the audience, as described above, is the first phase of a process known as *instructional analysis (IA)*, used by many instructors when developing the curriculum for their courses. The second phase of the process, determining the goals of the instructional experience, requires instructors to clearly articulate what they want their learners *to be able to do* upon completion of the instruction. Goal analysis involves detailing the various skills and sub-skills to be mastered and subject knowledge to be acquired. Most presenters do not need to conduct such a detailed goal-and-objective analysis unless they are providing formal instruction, but they should at least be able to clearly state what the audience *should be aware of* when leaving the presentation.

Think about this question for a moment: *What do you want your audience to know/think/do at the end of your presentation?* Can you write one succinct sentence that sums this up? Here are some examples:

1. I want my audience to create a five-slide PowerPoint presentation according to good multimedia guidelines.
2. I want to convince my audience to support my funding proposal.
3. I want my audience to believe they are leaders and to know some strategies for improving their leadership skills.

The sentences above clearly articulate the intended goal of each of the presentations described. Do not worry if you are not sure yet how you will ultimately 'answer' the question. I will ask you to repeat this exercise at a later point in the process, after you have become a bit more acquainted with your audience.

If you do feel that your one-sentence summary accurately captures the goal of your presentation, use it to generate 3–5 important points about the content of your presentation. Use your summary and list of important points to guide your initial approach to selecting the content for your presentation, but do not be afraid to change them later in the process if you decide they need editing to better meet your audience's needs.

Why articulate 3–5 points?

As we mentioned earlier in Part 1, our working memory has a number of limitations on its functioning: it can only handle a few elements at one time, we must pay attention to elements in order to process them, and the elements we do attend to are processed in one of two channels (visual or auditory) based on their format (images/speech).

Additionally, aside from the few who have eidetic (photographic) memories, most people must expend some mental effort in elaborating on presented material in order to encode it into long-term memory.

By elaborating, I mean the processes we use to understand material presented and to organize it into a coherent mental model. Students in a mathematics classroom rarely just listen to a lecture on quadratic equations and immediately have mastery over them; it is more likely that they must attend to the lecture, spend time with worked examples and solve practice problems in order to achieve mastery in solving these types of equations. This holds true for any material, simple or complex: in order to understand it and add it to long-term memory, it must be processed (elaborated upon) in working memory, though the time required for construction of a coherent mental model of the information varies from person to person.

Unfortunately, common presentations like the ones we give and attend at conferences often do not allow enough time for the audience to elaborate upon the material in order to fully understand it and add it to long-term memory. This is why presenters, when faced with an especially rich content area, should focus on *introducing* their presentation content to the audience and explicitly providing the structure (your 3–5 most important content points) of the content to the audience.

Conduct any necessary research

Depending on your topic and your experience with it, you may need to conduct some research to unearth facts to support your key points or to anticipate questions that might be posed. As this book's intended audience is librarians, I believe instructions on how to perform a literature review is unnecessary. However, let me remind you to include the bibliographic details for any sources you plan to cite. Include a slide containing a bibliography at the end of your presentation and/or include it as a handout for the audience. I also recommend including image credits, either as captions directly below the images themselves or else compiled in a list.

Summary

By the time you have completed gathering your logistical details, describing your audience and deciding how to structure your content, you will be well on your way to a more effective presentation. Taking the time to reflect on some of the questions posed above is a good way for you to focus on the needs of your audience and to increase the potential for better learning outcomes from your presentations. In Chapter 6 you will use your audience analysis and your stated goals to help you organize your content and create a written script which you will use to guide your visuals, construct your handouts and plan the delivery of your presentation.

6

Writing your script and creating your storyboards

Like any great film, television show or playhouse drama, a good presentation starts with a good script. A presentation script also describes much more than just the words that are spoken: the visuals you present, the tone you set, the message you communicate and the handouts you leave behind are all encompassed in your presentation script.

A useful approach to your script is to think of it first as if you were writing a technical report. From this report, you will select relevant content supporting your key points to structure your *spoken* remarks. If you take the time to create a solid written document during your preparations, you will not only have a rich source from which you can select your spoken content, but you will also have a comprehensive handout for audience members to take with them as a more in-depth review of the material you covered. This 'report' approach guides you to pursue a thorough treatment of the content of your presentation, allowing space for you to explore your content from a number of angles as if you had unlimited time with the audience.

Writing your script

You will use the details you have collected, your outline (summary sentence and 3–5 key points) and your research notes (all described in the previous chapter) to begin writing your script. I recommend you use pen and paper or your word processing program to structure your notes into a coherent document and avoid going directly to PowerPoint or Keynote at this stage of your preparation. As Jerry Weissman (2003: 43) and Edward Tufte (2003: 5) both point out, a linear, slide-by-slide approach too early in the process can short-circuit your thinking, reducing complex content to a series of superficial and generic bulleted lists. Use your experience writing formal academic documents to guide you and try not to plan too much at this stage about what you might speak or what visuals you might use (though you should keep a notepad handy to jot down particularly eloquent phrases or ideas for appropriate visuals that come to you as you write your script).

It was not until the last few years that I myself changed my own preparation habits to incorporate this step of explicitly approaching each and every presentation first and foremost as a written document. This method does take more time than starting your preparations directly in PowerPoint, but it can help you deliver a more effective presentation and help your audience learn more from it. Personally, it has helped reduce the frustration I often felt when preparing for a presentation: there was so much rich material I wanted to convey to the audience but the time allotted was insufficient. Knowing that I have a detailed and well-written document I can provide at the end of my presentation relieves that frustration for me.

Once you have written your first draft, go back and ask yourself the question I first posed to you in the previous chapter: *What do you want your audience to know/think/do at the end of your presentation?* Also, review your list of three to five main points. Is it time to alter your main points? Did you uncover more important aspects of the content you wish to emphasize? If you need to, write out a new one-sentence summary and revise your list of main points. Depending upon your writing style, you may complete several drafts of your report before settling on a final version. When you have completed your report (be sure to check it for grammar and spelling errors), you can turn your attention to your visuals by developing some storyboards for your presentation.

Storyboards

Storyboards are a series of drawings that serve to help film-makers and animators to pre-visualize and sequence a film, animated cartoon or other production. Most animated movies and movies with extensive special effects are often first depicted visually using storyboards. A series of storyboards serves as a graphic organizer for the production and can be usefully applied to the process of creating visuals for your presentation. It takes no special equipment of any kind, just blank paper and a pen, pencil or a set of coloured markers. You can easily create your own storyboard template by hand (Figure 6.1) or with a software program (Figure 6.2).

To create the PowerPoint storyboard template shown in Figure 6.2:

1. Launch PowerPoint and start a new presentation.

2. Insert two additional blank slides. (Click the *Insert Slide* icon or press [CTRL] + [M].)

Figure 6.1 A hand-drawn storyboard template

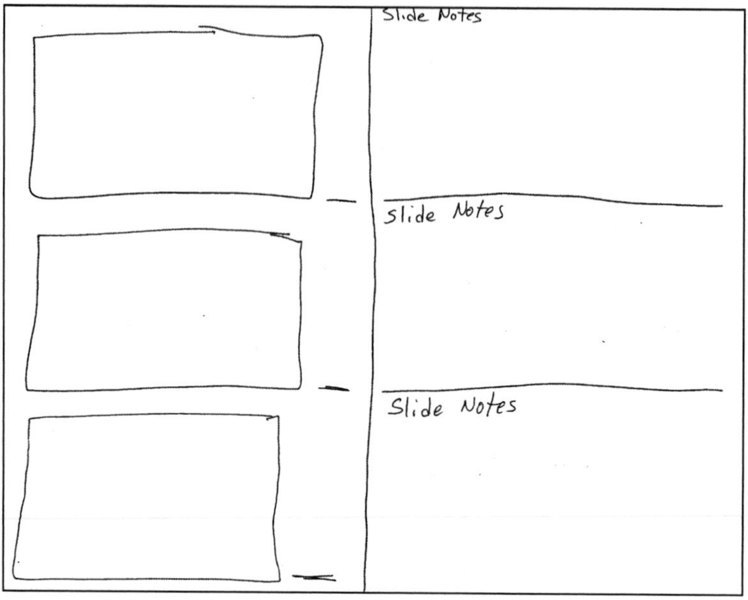

Figure 6.2 A storyboard template created using PowerPoint

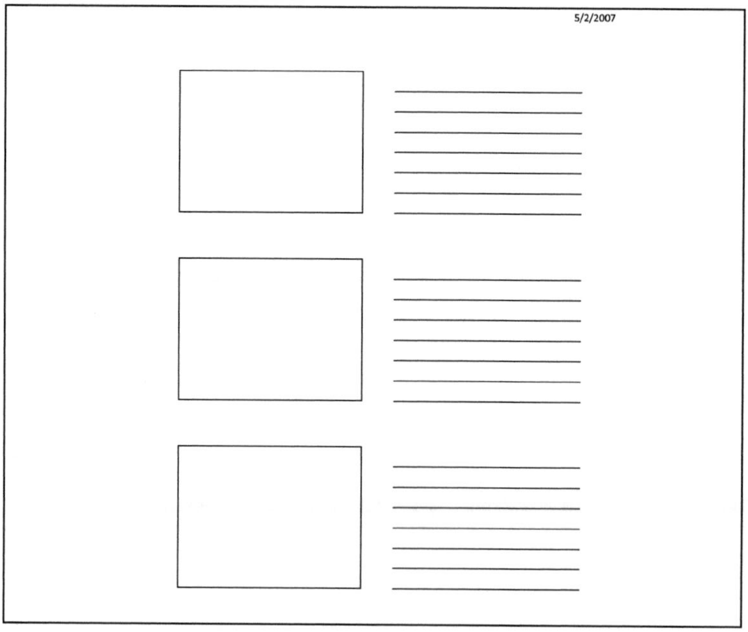

3. Press [CTRL] + [P] to open the *Print* dialogue box, then select 'Handouts' in the *Print What* option area.

4. Specify '3' *Slides per Page* and click **OK** to print.

5. Save the file for reuse.

There are many storyboard templates available free on the Web, and many stationery suppliers such as Levenger (*http://www.levenger.com*) also sell pre-printed storyboard pads with a wide variety of image frame sizes.

Storyboarding your presentation

Storyboarding for presentations is not as involved as storyboarding an animated film; you need only employ a few easy techniques to get results. Start with your first slide, your 'title slide'. Write the title in the centre of your first frame and your name below it. Sketch out any graphics you might include on your title slide (see Figure 6.3).

Figure 6.3 A sample title slide storyboard

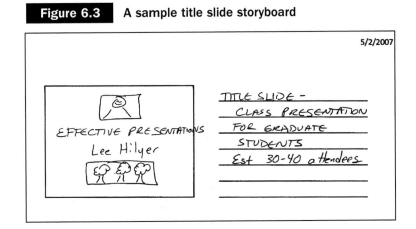

Next, consult your script to begin selecting chunks of content or important points to illustrate visually. Do you have an introductory story? If so, is there an image that 'summarizes' it? Are there common visual metaphors your audience understands that would relate to script content? Are you describing processes and/or procedures? These can often be illustrated with a static or animated diagram (see Figure 6.4). Sketch the diagram as best you can; you will use another software program (such as PowerPoint) to create the final version. Continue this process until you have created storyboards for all of the visuals in your

Figure 6.4   Some sample slide storyboards

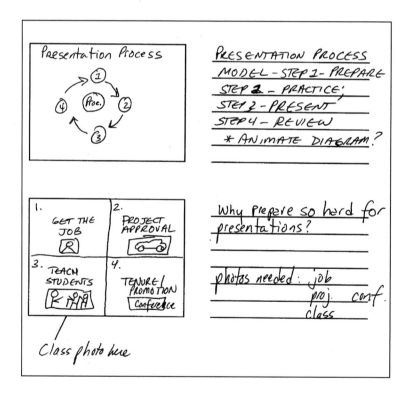

presentation. Once you have completed a set of storyboards, set them aside for a bit (a few hours to several days). When you begin again, review your storyboards and edit as needed.

Summary

For many of you, creating storyboards will be a new experience. Even if you doubt your artistic skills, you can certainly draw simple shapes and stick figures. The point of this process is for you to begin thinking visually about your content rather than verbally as you did when writing your script. The first and most important of Mayer's multimedia principles (as mentioned in Chapter 3) is that people learn better from words and pictures than from words alone.[1] Combining the two helps your audience to create richer and more robust mental models of your content, leading to better learning outcomes. Storyboarding can also be a very enjoyable part of the presentation process, where you can relax a little bit and have some fun drawing, just like you did when you were in primary school. In the next chapter, you will convert those storyboards to actual presentation slides.

Note

1. See also the *picture superiority effect* (pictures are remembered better than words) (Lidwell et al., 2003: 152).

Suggested further reading

Atkinson, C. (2005) *Beyond Bullet Points: Using Microsoft PowerPoint to Create Presentations That Inform, Motivate, and Inspire*. Redmond, WA: Microsoft Press.

Gordon, J. (2006) *Presentations That Change Minds: Strategies to Persuade, Convince, and Get Results*. New York: McGraw-Hill.

Sides, C.H. (1999) *How to Write and Present Technical Information*, 3rd edn. Phoenix, AZ: Oryx Press.

Weissman, J. (2003) *Presenting to Win: The Art of Telling Your Story*, special expanded edn. Upper Saddle River, NJ: FT Prentice Hall.

Wilson, A. (1998) *Handbook of Science Communication*. Bristol and Philadelphia: Institute of Physics Publishing.

7

Creating your slides

Presentation slides, such as those made with PowerPoint, Keynote or Impress, are the most common form of presentation visuals. Designing slides with multimedia learning and good design principles in mind can increase the effectiveness of your visuals and help achieve the desired goals for your presentation. The storyboards you drew earlier can now be used to help you create your slides. Rather than focusing on the capabilities of a particular software program, this chapter provides general recommendations for the visual design and construction of slides that are applicable to any slide presentation software. Appendices A–C provide more specific information on three widely used presentation software programs.

We discussed the multimedia principle that people learn better from words and pictures than from words alone in Part 1. The dual-channel nature of our working memory (one channel for processing visual information, another for processing auditory information) supports this principle. As you are using your storyboards to translate your written content into visual images and diagrams, you are, in effect, attempting to balance the load between the visual and auditory channels in the minds of your audience members, thus helping them to more efficiently use their processing resources to actively process your content in working memory. Use the techniques and sample slide layouts below to help you organize and present the content of your presentation so it can be more efficiently processed by your audience.

Slide layouts

Slide layouts are used to help structure and organize the informational content of a slide; they consist of multiple elements, such as text boxes and graphics that can easily be moved, resized, formatted and positioned on a customizable background. Each element serves as a 'container' that can hold different *content* (text, image, sound clip, movie file, chart, etc.) and which often performs a specific navigational or semantic (i.e. 'meaning') *function* for the slide content: headline, bullet point, body text, caption, etc.

Many software programs offer 'themes' or 'slide designs', which are coordinated sets of slide layouts you can use containing complementary colour schemes, related graphic elements and pre-positioned placeholders to structure and organize the information on your slide (see Figure 7.1). We will consider themes in more detail at the end of this chapter; however, my general recommendation is to first complete all of your slides using simple black text on a white background. This helps keep you focused on the content of the slide rather than its formatting.

As a reader, you navigate texts such as journal articles, books and web pages using elements of *page layout*. For instance, you can easily turn to the beginning of this chapter and identify the chapter title by its prominence on the page. You know that page numbers are often found in the margins

Figure 7.1 A slide layout with placeholders for text and graphics

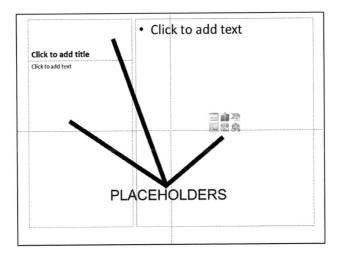

of a page and can be used to navigate through the text to the specific page desired. Veteran readers employ these navigational guides automatically, the necessary mental procedures for reading having been elaborated upon and practised countless times previously. It is doubly important for presenters to pay careful attention to the layout of their slides, because unlike readers of a printed document, who can use the document's built-in navigational tools at their leisure, audience members usually have only the slide on display to guide them.

Recommended sequence of slides

A common sequence of slides for a presentation usually includes a *title* slide, an *agenda* or *outline* slide, and a subsequent series of *content* slides. I recommend a slightly more detailed sequence of slide layouts to use for most of the presentation situations you might encounter, as shown in Table 7.1.

Table 7.1	Sequence of slides for a typical presentation

1. Title slide
2. Agenda slide
3. Key points slide
4. Bumper slide
5. Content slide (various layouts)
6. Key points review slide
7. Question and answer slide
8. Ending slide
9. Bibliography/image credits slides

Below are detailed descriptions of each layout and several sample slides for each type.

The title slide

A title slide is your presentation's 'first impression': it is the first slide the audience will see and it sets the visual 'tone' for the presentation to follow. 'You never get a second chance to make a first impression,' goes the familiar adage, and your title slide is no exception – make an impact with your title slide the moment your presentation begins. Title slides are probably the easiest to create since you need only include minimal elements (title, your name (and affiliation), an image and perhaps the date) yet they allow for great freedom of expression and creativity. Look at these examples in Figure 7.2(a)–(c).

Figure 7.2(a) Sample title slide layout

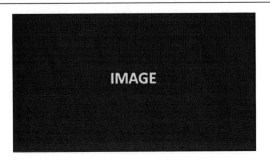

Figure 7.2(b) Modified title slide layout

Figure 7.2(c) Modified title slide layout using a photograph as a background

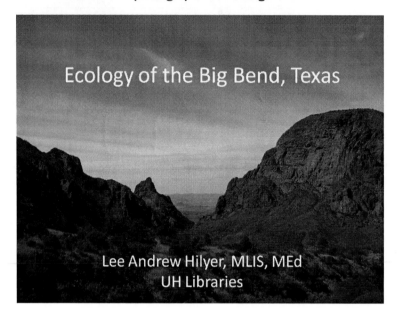

Each variation includes the necessary elements listed above yet is flexible enough for a variety of situations. Using a 'full-bleed' photograph as the slide background (Figure 7.2(c)) is one easy technique to incorporate into your own title slide layouts.

The agenda (outline) slide

The agenda or outline slide is a 'road map' to your presentation content, either arranged chronologically (e.g. 'Today's Agenda') or in a particular sequence (e.g. 'Course Outline') (see Figure 7.3(a)–(b)). When properly supported by the speaker, it provides the audience with the structure and sequence of the content ahead, a kind of 'cognitive scaffolding' that they can use to assist them as they begin building the necessary mental models needed for long-term storage.

Figure 7.3(a)   Sample agenda slide layout

> ### Your Agenda Might Look Like This ...
>
> 1. About Me
>
> 2. What I've Been Doing This Year
>
> 3. Reasons Why I Deserve a Summer Vacation
>
> 4. What I Will Be Doing on My Summer Vacation
>
> 5. Travel Timeline
>
> 6. Places I Would Like to Spend My Summer Vacation

Figure 7.3(b)   Sample agenda slide using photographs

This summer, I will be travelling all across Europe!

United Kingdom   **France**

Germany

The 'key points' slide

The key points of your presentation form the structural 'frame' of your content (see Figure 7.4) and are intended to help the audience grasp the overall structure of the presentation and be able to recognize the key points as they are explained and reinforced through the content slides to follow. Because of the limited duration of a presentation, emphasizing the key points helps the audience to know where to focus their attention and where to apply their cognitive resources.

Figure 7.4   Sample 'key points' slide

Three Things to Remember About How We Learn

1. Working memory has **two channels** (visual/auditory) for receiving and processing information.
2. Working memory has **limited** capacity to store information.
3. Incoming information is **actively processed** in working memory to organize it into a coherent mental representation.

Remember to limit your key points to three or less for short presentations (30 minutes or less) and four to five points for longer ones (45 minutes or more). Including more key points than the audience can handle increases the potential for cognitive overload and a decrease in learning.

The 'bumper' slide

A 'bumper' slide is used between sequences of slides dealing with different content sections (e.g. 'Methodology', 'Results', 'Conclusions'). It serves to orient the audience to the content to follow, encourages the activation of prior knowledge related to the upcoming content and continues the 'scaffolding' begun with the agenda slide. Two options for bumper slides include using a modified agenda slide, as shown in Figure 7.5(a), or using a 'title card' layout as shown in Figure 7.5(b).

Figure 7.5(a) Sample 'bumper' slide layout (modified agenda layout)

Agenda / Key Points

About Me

What I've Been Doing This Year

Reasons Why I Deserve a Summer Vacation

What I Will Be Doing on My Summer Vacation

Travel Timeline

Places I Would Like to Spend My Summer Vacation

Figure 7.5(b) Sample 'bumper' slide layout (title card layout)

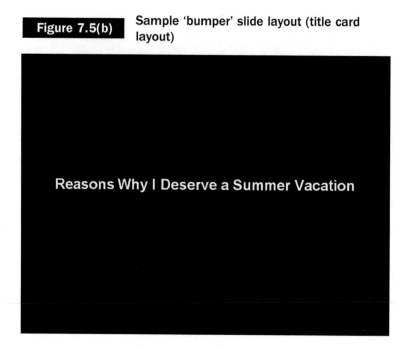

Reasons Why I Deserve a Summer Vacation

Content slides (multiple layouts)

The majority of your presentation visuals will be content slides, where you present the evidence in support of each of your key points. You will source the material for these slides from your written document and your storyboards and need only master a few techniques which you can combine in endless variations across myriad presentation situations to ensure effective visuals.

In general, a content slide *should be able to stand alone and communicate a complete thought* to the viewer. This is a common failing of presentation slides today. Cryptic, short-phrase headlines and incomplete bullet points fail to communicate the complete thought to the viewer. To better connect with your audience, your slides should utilize the same structures and methods employed by media formats (newspapers, television and movies) already familiar to the viewer.

Start with the headline

According to research conducted by Michael Alley and his colleagues (2005, 2006), using a sentence-style headline is more effective in helping the audience retain information presented than the more common short-phrase title usually found on most slides. Using no more than two lines, the sentence-style headline should succinctly state the main idea of the slide *and* present a complete thought to the viewer. Left-align the text and begin the sentence at the top left of the slide, as in Figure 7.6.

Figure 7.6   Content slide layout using a sentence headline

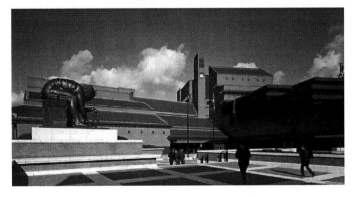

I will first be travelling to the United Kingdom to visit the British Library.

This is the new British Library at St Pancras.

Add a relevant image

Below your headline, use an appropriate image or piece of clip art to visually explain the headline above. If the topic is more abstract, consider locating an image that can serve as a visual metaphor of the idea. The concept of *growth*, for example, can be illustrated with images and clip art from the worlds of agriculture, human development, finance and many more.

Use *either* clip art *or* photographs in your presentations, not both (see Figure 7.7(a) and (b)). The use of consistent imagery contributes to the professional appearance of your slides. Sometimes images can be used alone without a headline to great dramatic effect. If necessary, add a caption to the photograph documenting its copyright status, or, in the case of a chart or other statistical graph, add a line or two detailing the primary assumption behind the graph.

Figure 7.7(a)   **Clip art should be used in light-hearted and less serious presentations**

Figure 7.7(b) Use photographs whenever possible to enhance the visual impact of your presentation

Photographs

Chisos Mountain Range, Big Bend National Park, Texas	Pecos River, West Texas

Remove most of the text from your slides

All presenters should avoid text-heavy slides, as illustrated in Figure 7.8. As discussed in Part 1, displayed text is partly

Figure 7.8 AVOID text-filled slides

Sarbanes-Oxley Act of 2002

- Section 302 requires certifications of each quarterly and annual report by the CEO and CFO
- Section 404 requires an annual *internal control* report by management stating the responsibility of management for establishing and maintaining adequate *internal control* for financial reporting, and providing an assessment of the effectiveness of the *internal control* structure and procedures for financial reporting
- The external auditor is required to attest to and report on management's assessment pursuant to standards developed by the Public Company Accounting Oversight Board (PCAOB)

processed in the auditory channel of working memory, competing with spoken content for the channel's limited resources. Remove any text from a slide that can be incorporated into your spoken remarks or depicted through an image or diagram. See 'using text in visuals' later in this chapter for more guidance.

Redisplay the 'key points' slide

After presenting all of your content slides, you will then redisplay your original key points slide and verbally summarize them again for your audience. This gives the audience a final chance to elaborate on the content, linking facts from your content slides to your important key points. Repeat presented examples rather than using new ones when verbally summarizing your key points.

The 'question and answer' slide

In many situations, the presentation itself is often followed by a question-and-answer period, in which the audience has a chance to interact with the presenter one to one. The question and answer slide should be simple, usually containing just the word 'Questions?' in large type, like a bumper slide. It can also be combined with an 'ending slide' as shown in Figure 7.9.

The end (almost)

Your penultimate slide should be an 'ending' slide and will serve as a visual cue to the official end of the presentation. It should thank the audience for their attention and should provide your contact information (if appropriate and/or you have not already done so). A useful technique for an ending slide is to repeat the same image from your title slide (if appropriate). Conclude with any final remarks, and receive your applause while the ending slide is displayed.

Figure 7.9   Sample 'ending' slide

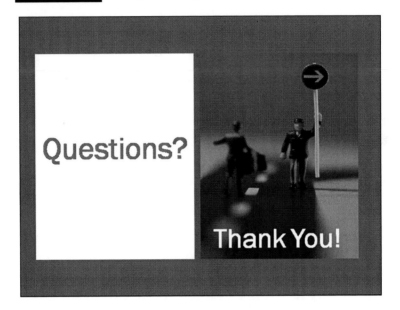

The bibliography and image credits slides

Compile a bibliography of the sources you used and/or list your image credits on the final slide(s) of your presentation. Bibliographies are a normal part of scholarly research and your presentations should be properly documented, just as your essays and journal articles would be. Following the bibliography, list any image credits as appropriate. These final two slides do not necessarily need to be displayed to the live audience, but can be especially useful if you plan to distribute the presentation later (by e-mail or website posting, for example), so that your 'virtual' viewers can seek out the resources you used.

Using themes/slide designs

Once you have crafted all of your slides, you can consider additional formatting that may help reinforce your intended message to the audience. Themes can add to the professional appearance of your presentation, but must be used carefully and in accordance with good design and multimedia guidelines. Keep in mind these general guidelines for working with themes:

- Design elements should not detract from your content nor project a mood or feeling contrary to your intended message.
- Avoid outlandish colour schemes or overwrought animations.
- Text should maintain high visibility and simplicity, i.e. no drop-shadows, no three-dimensional effects, no garish colours.

Using text in visuals

Even though I encourage you throughout this book to replace text on your slides with images and diagrams, a proper amount of text on a slide ensures understanding without inducing cognitive overload. This section will briefly provide you with some guidelines on how best to format the text of your slides. We will begin with a brief explanation of *fonts*.

What are fonts?

The words *font* and *typeface* are often used interchangeably. Fonts are a set of letters, numbers and punctuation marks all having the same visual style, expressed in their dimensions (width and height), their proportions and any ornamentation added to them. Different fonts have different proportions, styling and other characteristics. You should give some thought to the fonts you choose in your presentation, as they often make an impression on the viewer, as images and colours do. You want to be sure that the font you select conveys the proper impression you want the audience to have of you and your topic.

Serif vs. sans-serif

The two main categories of fonts are *serif* and *sans-serif*. There are also what are known as 'script' and 'display' fonts, but these categories of fonts are not usually recommended for use in presentations. Display fonts can sometimes be used to great effect in a presentation, but script fonts should be avoided in a presentation because their thin lines and ornamentation affect their legibility on presentation slides.

Serif fonts have small lines or marks protruding from the ends of letters often thought to be a holdover from when letters were carved onto buildings (i.e. the chisel marks left behind at the end of letters). These serifs were incorporated into metal typefaces as printing developed and still persist today in digital form (see Figure 7.10). Times New Roman, Trajan, Palatino Linotype and Clarendon are all examples of serif typefaces.

Sans-serif (the French word 'sans' means 'without') are typefaces without serifs on their letters. Arial, Calibri (a new Microsoft font found in Office 2007) and the popular Helvetica are all examples of sans-serif fonts (see Figure 7.11). Sans-serif fonts are often viewed as having a more 'modern' feel than serif fonts.

Figure 7.10　The difference between serif and sans-serif fonts

What's the Difference?

A a **A a**

Times New Roman　　　　**Franklin Gothic Demi**

SERIF　　　　　　　　　**SANS SERIF**

Figure 7.11　Some serif and sans-serif font options

Serif vs. Sans Serif

Some serif fonts:	Some **sans serif** fonts:
Times New Roman	Arial
Baskerville Old Face	Century Gothic
Bookman Old Style	Franklin Gothic
Palatino Linotype	Tahoma

Which one should I use?

The answer is, 'It depends.' Conventional wisdom holds that serif fonts are generally considered more legible than sans-serif fonts, especially for longer passages (such as those found in a book or journal article), yet a review of the published literature by Alex Poole (2005) indicates that most studies comparing serif and sans-serif fonts find no significant differences in legibility between the two. For more formal occasions, a serif font is probably best, while more informal presentations or technology presentations will benefit from a modern sans-serif font.

Technical considerations for fonts

Unless you convert your slides to images (JPEG or PNG format) or to Adobe Acrobat PDF format, you will need to be careful when selecting a font to use in your slides. Some of the fonts available on your computer may have been installed with another program (such as Adobe Photoshop) and it *may not* be possible to embed them into your presentation. If you are not delivering your presentation using the same computer you prepared on, you may find that PowerPoint or Keynote has substituted a generic font for the one you originally chose, resulting in a messy and unprofessional-looking presentation. Most presenters only discover this problem the hard way – about five minutes before they are scheduled to deliver their presentation!

To avoid this problem, select one of the default fonts that are installed with your presentation software or office suite, though I recommend using something other than Times Roman (serif) or Arial (sans-serif). Both of these fonts have been overused in PowerPoint presentations. *Tahoma* or *Verdana* are both excellent sans-serif choices, and *Palatino*

Linotype and *Garamond* are two lesser-used serif options. Microsoft Office users should stick to either the default fonts installed as part of Windows or the fonts installed as part of the Microsoft Office system. Apple Macintosh (Mac) users should stick to the fonts installed as part of the computer's operating system (currently OS X).

Size and weight of fonts

For formatting text on your slides, the smallest type size I recommend is 16 point (pt). It can be read from the back of most average-sized classrooms and smaller hotel meeting rooms. If possible, you should test the readability of text *beforehand* in a room similar to the size of the one you will be presenting in. If you are going to be presenting in a large room, increase your smallest text size to 18 pt or 20 pt. On the upper end of the scale, you probably need to set text no larger than 48 pt. Some text on bumper slides might be as large as 64 pt or 72 pt. Text sized at 32 pt is adequate for most slide headlines, while remaining text should usually be set in 24 pt. You should also consider factors such as the size of the room, the lighting conditions and your audience's needs when sizing type.

Selecting a font colour

The colour combination familiar to most audiences is black text on a white background. The reverse (white text on a black background) is another simple yet effective colour combination. The general recommendation for all font colour/background colour combinations is to place *dark* text on a *light* background and, conversely, *light* text on a *dark* background. (see Figure 7.12(a)–(b)).

Figure 7.12(a)   Dark text placed on a light slide background

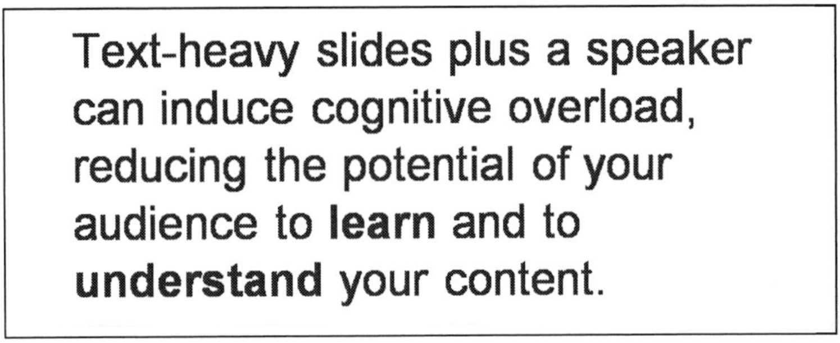

Text-heavy slides plus a speaker can induce cognitive overload, reducing the potential of your audience to **learn** and to **understand** your content.

Figure 7.12(b)   Light text placed on a dark slide background

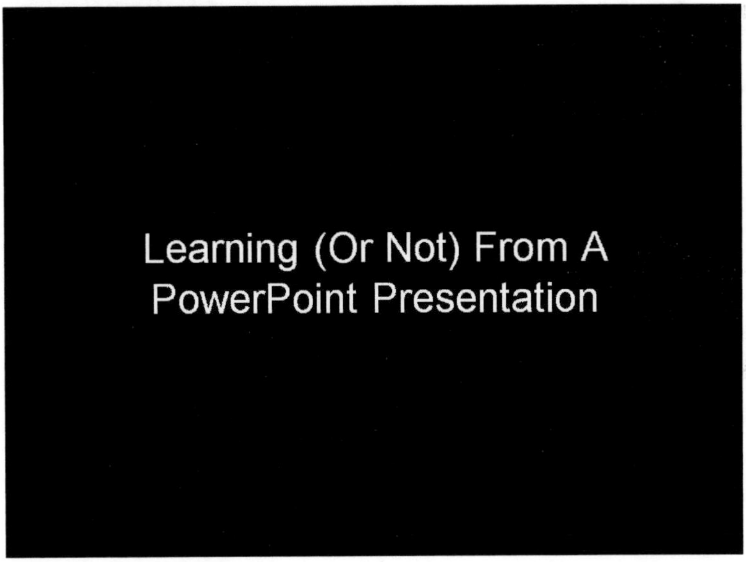

Learning (Or Not) From A PowerPoint Presentation

Using images

Transforming textual content into images can help balance the cognitive load between the visual channel and the auditory channel, and have a powerful effect on learning. When combined with relevant spoken content from the presenter, audience members can integrate both verbal and visual information into a more complete mental model of the content you are presenting. Similarly, diagrams and statistical displays, again accompanied by relevant spoken content, provide a richer learning experience than an endless series of text-filled slides.

Types of images

Images can be *representational*: they attempt to be an accurate and faithful depiction of something. Photographs, screenshots and scanned documents are examples of representational images. Images can also be *figurative* or *metaphorical*, standing in for abstract concepts such as 'customer service', 'Inter-Library Loan', 'user-centred' and the like. Clip art and other types of abstract illustrations are good examples of figurative images.

Technical considerations for image files

Images can instantly improve the quality and effectiveness of your presentation, provided they are relevant and targeted to the content you are presenting. However, even if you have selected relevant images, their impact will be diminished if they are of poor quality or are adjusted incorrectly. Your main consideration should be the size of the image you want to use and the image's *resolution*.

Size refers to the physical dimensions of the image taken and *resolution* refers to the number of pixels (picture elements) that comprise the image – the more pixels per inch, the higher the resolution (and size) of the image. In general, use the highest resolution (often expressed in dpi (dots per inch)) image available to you. It is better to reduce the size of a large, high-resolution image than to enlarge a low-resolution image. When enlarged, low-resolution images often show pixilation, also known as the 'jaggies', where the individual pixels that make up the image become apparent to the viewer. All major slide presentation software packages support the most common image file formats (JPEG, GIF and PNG). PowerPoint and other presentation programs also enable you to edit images directly, performing such actions as cropping the image, adjusting its transparency or transforming it from colour to black and white (a very dramatic technique when executed well).

Sources for images

Images for use in your presentations can be obtained from a wide variety of sources: your own camera, from stock photo agencies, from government and educational agencies, and from the Web at large. You can also create your own screenshots (useful for software training) or scan your own objects or documents using a scanner. Remember to look for the highest-resolution images you can find.

Copyright issues

Many stock photo agencies include language in their licences allowing use of the image in a slide presentation, but be sure to check the agreement before you purchase an image. If instructed by the licence, include the copyright statement as a caption or in the list of image credits at the end of your presentation. Many museums and libraries allow presenters to use images from their collections for non-commercial, educational use (such as a conference presentation). Using images taken freely from the Web may or may not be permitted under the copyright laws in your country. Consult with the relevant copyright authority in your country for more information on using images in your presentations.

Diagrams and statistical displays

If an appropriate photo or piece of clip art cannot be located to represent text, diagrams can be a useful way to 'transform' textual content into an effective visual. For example, a list of steps (Figure 7.13) can be graphically represented as a circular process diagram (Figure 7.14).

Notice that the diagram in Figure 7.14 is circular, implying that each step is part of a continuous cycle. The cyclical nature of the process is lost in the bulleted list in Figure 7.13.

Figure 7.13 Slide using *text* to describe a cyclical process

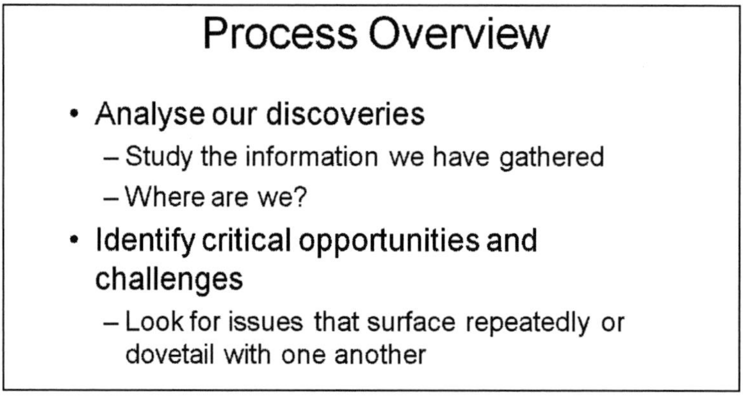

Process Overview

- Analyse our discoveries
  - Study the information we have gathered
  - Where are we?
- Identify critical opportunities and challenges
  - Look for issues that surface repeatedly or dovetail with one another

Figures 7.15 and 7.16 provide a further example. While the graphic timeline (Figure 7.16) represents the same information as the sequence of text slides (Figure 7.15), the graphic version not only provides a complete visual that can be comprehended as a whole, but also saves time by fitting information that was originally presented on three slides

Figure 7.14 Slide using a *diagram* to describe a cyclical process

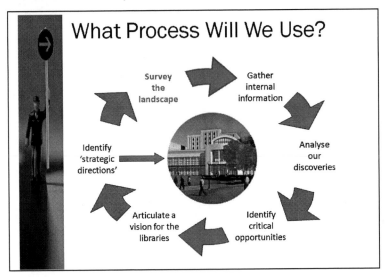

Figure 7.15 Slide with timeline represented as text

Timeline

- January – February 2006
  - Meet with committees and departments
  - Brainstorm as a committee
  - Analyse our data
- March 2006
  - Identify critical opportunities and challenges
- April 2006
  - Vision for our 3-year horizon
- May – June 2006
  - Identify strategic directions for the libraries
  - June 30 completion date
- July 2006 – ???

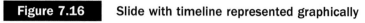

Figure 7.16 Slide with timeline represented graphically

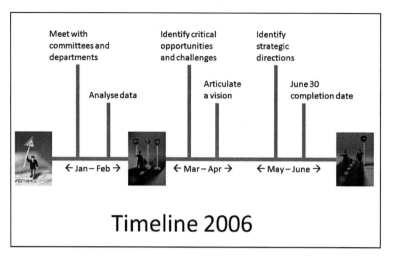

into one. When converting text into diagrams, be sure that the diagram's arrangement properly organizes and represents your content. Cyclical processes are often best represented by circular diagrams, whereas more finite processes or structures can be represented with a more linear one such as a flowchart.

Statistical displays (graphs and charts)

Statistical displays serve as excellent options for visually depicting numerical content in your presentation. Simple graphs and charts are often backed by hundreds or thousands of data points, which can be provided to the audience on paper. Resist the temptation to insert a spreadsheet into a slide. Instead, invest some time in graphing and charting your data, then select the best to include in your slides. You are often limited in time during a presentation, and an accurate and reliable chart or graph conveys more information simply and more elegantly than row upon row of raw or semi-polished data. If you need to include additional data tables to support your key points, do so in printed format which the audience members can later analyse at their own pace.

Accurate and reliable statistical displays

As in any scholarly endeavour, the conclusions you draw in your presentation should be supported by evidence which is valid, accurate and reliable. Statistical displays should be constructed so as to be quickly and accurately interpreted by the audience. Graphs and charts should be rigorously revised to remove all but the most relevant information, which Edward Tufte refers to as maximizing the data–ink ratio (Tufte, 2001, 2003).

By default, many spreadsheet and slide presentation software programs create complex, multi-coloured and totally cluttered graphs. Thankfully, you have extensive control over formatting options and can adjust your graphs to emphasize the data and minimize any irrelevant or extraneous information. Learn the options available to you in your software programs, and rigorously remove all but the most important data and information from the graph. Figure 7.17 shows an example of an unaltered chart created using Microsoft Excel while Figure 7.18 provides a second version where 'chartjunk' (see Tufte, 2004) has been minimized.

If you need to explain any assumptions or other information about the data you are presenting, be sure to explain these verbally, as a footnote for the graph and as part of the handout including the additional data tables. This ensures the audience receives the full and complete analysis of your findings.

Figure 7.17   Sample chart

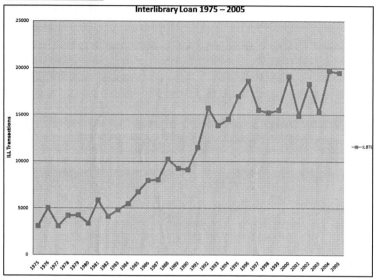

Source: Data taken from the *Association of Research Libraries Statistics – Interactive Edition* (*http://fisher.lib.virginia.edu/arl/*).

Figure 7.18   Sample chart edited to remove 'chartjunk'

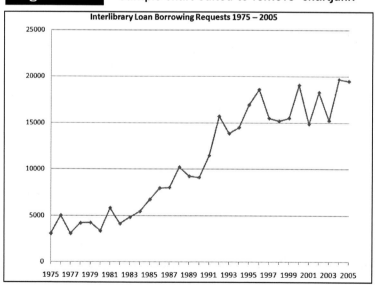

Source: Data taken from the *Association of Research Libraries Statistics – Interactive Edition* (*http://fisher.lib.virginia.edu/arl/*).

Summary

By incorporating a few of the techniques and guidelines described above into your slide creation process, you can improve the quality of your presentation visuals and increase the potential for meaningful learning by your audience. The above guidelines draw their inspiration from many sources: theories of learning and instruction, graphic and information design principles and scholarly tradition. Below you will find a list of suggested resources to help you explore in more detail the topics covered above.

You may have noticed that slides with bulleted lists are scarce in this book; this is intentional. It is the least effective slide layout and can easily be eliminated in favour of more effective slides using images or diagrams or by simply *speaking* the content. In the next chapter, we will turn our attention to designing effective presentation handouts. Then, in Chapter 9, you will integrate your spoken content, your visuals and your handouts into a complete presentation through an iterative process of practice and revision.

Suggested further reading

Clark, R.C. and Lyons, C.C. (2004) *Graphics for Learning: Proven Guidelines for Planning, Designing, and Evaluating Visuals in Training Materials.* San Francisco: Pfeiffer; Chichester: John Wiley.

Few, S. (2004) *Show Me the Numbers: Designing Tables and Graphs to Enlighten*, 1st edn. Oakland, CA: Analytics Press.

Irwin, T. and Terberg, J. (2004) *Perfect Medical Present-*

ations: Creating Effective Powerpoint Presentations for the Healthcare Professional. Edinburgh and New York: Churchill Livingstone.

Lidwell, W., Holden, K. and Butler, J. (2003) *Universal Principles of Design.* Gloucester, MA: Rockport.

Manning, A. and Amare, N. (2005) *Using Visual Rhetoric to Avoid PowerPoint Pitfalls.* Paper presented at the IEEE International Professional Communication Conference.

Stewart, M. (2006) *Launching the Imagination. A Comprehensive Guide to Two-Dimensional Design,* 2nd edn. Boston: McGraw-Hill.

8

Creating effective handouts

The presentation handout is the third important component of an effective presentation experience for the audience. It serves as a written summary of the presentation, can provide additional explanatory content for the audience to review later at its leisure, provide further explanation of statistical analyses (data tables, equations, etc.) and direct audience members to additional resources beyond those covered in the spoken presentation. It can also encourage more elaborate and effortful processing of information, which can lead to better retention of the material and to the increased potential of its use in other situations (see Chapter 1 for more information on learning, retention and transfer).

Mostly, though, the number of presentations accompanied by effective handouts is small. Many presenters unwittingly create handouts with little or no value, amounting to a waste of time and resources. Figure 8.1 is an example of a common presentation handout.

As a recipient of these types of handouts, do you really take notes that you can decipher later? Can you easily read the text in the reduced slide images? Probably not. Without the context of the speaker's spoken narration, the slides by themselves (or accompanied by incoherent notes) often cannot be easily understood, or worse, can easily be

| Figure 8.1 | A common format for presentation handouts |

Source: Handout from a presentation created by Nancy Linden. Reproduced with permission.

misinterpreted. A handout should be a *supplement* to the presentation and be able to stand on its own.

If you used the process described in Chapter 6, your handout should be well on its way to completion, or may already be complete. You may only need to do some minor edits on your original script for it to serve as an effective handout. Alternatively, based on your rehearsals of the presentation, you may find that the handout needs to be expanded to cover additional, related material that you will not have time to cover live.

Handout formats

My first choice is always the simplest: a standard, properly formatted document similar to a technical report or, for more informal presentations, similar to a newsletter. It might contain graphs or photographs, or it might be text only (though as mentioned earlier, using text and pictures together often yields better learning outcomes, so try to get some pictures or diagrams into your handouts as well).

My second choice is to print a handout using the 'Notes Pages' option, which is available in most presentation software programs (see Figure 8.2).

Figure 8.2   'Notes Pages' handout format

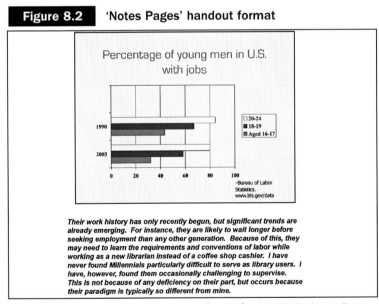

Source: Handout from a presentation by Catherine W. Essinger. Reproduced with permission.

A third choice, if you have not already written a report or if you wish to design a different document, is to send the text and images from your presentation into a word processor. Many slide presentation programs allow you to export slide images and text to another software program. PowerPoint 2007, for example, has a 'Create Handouts in Word' option that creates a new document using your slides and notes. A two-column table layout is used with slide images in the left column and text from the Notes pane on the right.

Figure 8.3 Handout created using the 'Create Handouts in Word' option in PowerPoint

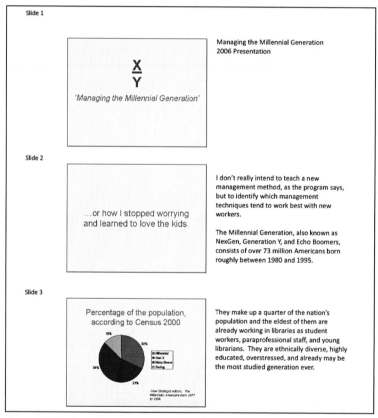

Source: Handout from a presentation by Catherine W. Essinger. Reproduced with permission.

A more elaborate choice, and one I use for lengthy instruction sessions, was suggested by Edward Tufte in his 2004 self-published essay entitled *The Cognitive Style of PowerPoint*. It uses one 11" × 17" (A3) sheet of paper folded in half to form an 8.5" × 11" (A4)-sized brochure with a front and back page and two inside pages (see Figure 8.4).

The four-page format allows for extensive treatment of content in a compact and portable package. I have found that it provides me with extensive space to summarize my instruction as well as provide tips and how-to directions so that the handout can be kept and reused by the audience member later.

You can create this type of handout in Word or another word processing program by using the multiple text columns feature:

1. Create a blank document and adjust the size of the document to A3 (11" × 17"; Tabloid) and change its orientation to *landscape*.

2. Split each page into two columns of equal size (do not use a table).

3. Type (or paste) the document contents in the following page order: 4|1, 2|3.

4. Follow the instructions for your particular printer to print the document so that when folded, the pages follow the correct sequence.

This can be a bit tricky and requires patience, especially when determining which way to feed paper into your printer. You can also use Adobe InDesign or Quark Xpress page layout software to create this type of handout. It is little used by presenters and well worth the extra effort it requires as it can provide a large amount of content in a convenient format for browsing.

Figure 8.4 Handout in four-page format (A3 or 11" × 17")

Class Activities Continued

Activity 4 – Animation Schemes

o Locate your **Bulleted List** slide in your presentation and click it to make it the active slide.
o Click the bullet points section once to make it active.
o In the Task Pane, select **Slide Design – Animation Schemes**. (These are pre-set animation schemes for you to use in your presentation).
   o Note that animation effects run the gamut from subtle to exciting. Click on a scheme in the list to see a preview. If you hover your mouse over a scheme in the list, a Tool Tip will appear listing the various animations that PowerPoint will apply to titles and body text on your slide. Some schemes also include a transition effect.

Note: Custom Animation (including Motion Paths) will be covered in the Advanced PowerPoint class. Check the Library's website for the class schedule.

Activity 5 – Transitions

o Return to the Title slide of your presentation.
o In the Task Pane, select **Slide Transition**.
o Select the transition effect you would like to use and select a speed (Slow/Medium/Fast).
o Click **Apply to All Slides**.

Note: Transitions can be applied to a single slide for emphasis, or they can be applied to every slide in a presentation.

Activity 6 – Slide Show Controls

o To watch your slide show, press <F5>, or choose **Slide Show** from the **View** menu.
o Press the space bar or the right arrow (→) key to advance to the next slide.
o Experiment with some of the other available slide show controls (see Tips & Techniques sheet).

Bibliography

Bird, Linda. "15 Top PowerPoint Tips." PC Magazine, December 30th, 2003. 70-72. (http://www.pcmag.com)

Hadfield-Law, Lisa. Effective Presentations for Health Care Professionals. Oxford: Butterworth-Heinemann, 1999. In UT-Central, UT-M.D. Anderson, and UTMB libraries.

Online Training Solutions, Inc. Step-by-Step: Microsoft Office PowerPoint 2003. Redmond, WA: Microsoft Press, 2004.

"Presentation Tips from Dale Carnegie." http://office.microsoft.com/assistance/2002/articles/poTipsForPresenting.aspx

Rose, Catherine S. and Patricia Dewdney. Communicating Professionally, 2nd ed. New York: Neal-Schuman, 1998. In TMC Library.

Siwinski, Carol. "Rubric for Multimedia Presentation." http://www.nd.edu/~learning/powerpoint/ (Note especially the section entitled "Workshop Handouts (PDF)"

EFFECTIVE POWERPOINT PRESENTATIONS 2005

Description

This class provides you with a basic introduction to creating your own slide shows using PowerPoint 2003. *Familiarity with computers and with Windows is required.*

Class Activities

Activity 1 – Getting Started

Launch PowerPoint by either double-clicking the PowerPoint icon on your desktop, or by selecting it from the **Start>Programs** menu. Spend a minute or two looking around the interface and viewing the various menu options available. Note the Task Pane on the right-hand side of the screen. (If you do not see the Task Pane, select **View>Normal** from the menu, or press CTRL + F1.

Activity 2 – Creating Slides

A. Title Slide

In PowerPoint 2003, a title slide layout will automatically be selected for you.

o Enter a title for your presentation.
o Enter your name in the **subtitle** section.
o Press CTRL+S (or go to File>Save from the menu) and save your file to the DESKTOP.

Congratulations! You have just created your first PowerPoint slide!

B. Bulleted List Slide

The Bulleted List layout is the most-used (and over-used) of any PowerPoint layout.

o In the **Task Pane (Slide Layout)**, select the Bulleted List slide layout (Tool tip says: "Title and Text"). Use the drop-down menu to select the **Insert New Slide** option.
o Enter a title for this slide: [Steps in Custom Animation].
o In the lower section, enter the following bullet points:
   o [Select the item you wish to animate.]
   o [Select effects.]
   o [Specify the order and timing of effects.]
   o [Preview.]
o In the 3rd bullet, make the words [order] and [timing] bold.
o Change the bullets to a numbered list by selecting the bulleted list text area, then selecting the **Numbering** icon in the **Formatting** toolbar.

C. Text & Content Slide

o In the Task Pane **(Slide Layout)**, select a Text & Content slide layout (Tool tip says: "Title, Text and Content"). Use the drop-down menu to select the **Insert New Slide** option.
o Enter a title for this slide: [Content Layouts]

Inserting Text:

o In the text section, enter the following bullet points (Hint: To complete a multi-level list of bullet points, you will need to turn on the Outlining Toolbar. Go to **View>Toolbars** and select **Outlining.**):
   o [Use pre-defined content layouts for slides with multiple elements]
      • [Text]
         • [Titles]
            • [Multimedia]
               • [Photos]

Spring 2005 – Lee Andrew Hilyer, MLIS (lhilyer@library.tmc.edu)

- [Clip Art]
- [Movies]
- [Sounds]

Inserting Multimedia (Clip Art; Photos; Music; Movies; Etc.):

Notice that the content placeholder has six (6) different icons. Hover your mouse over each icon to see its function.

o Click the **Insert Picture** icon.
o Insert one (1) piece of clip art into your slide.

If you want to insert additional media objects, select an option from the **Insert** menu, **or**, you can select the **Clip Art** section of the Task Pane by choosing it from the drop-down menu.

D. Inserting a Chart

You can use PowerPoint's built-in charting function to create simple charts and graphs. For very detailed visual displays of statistical information, consider creating the chart in another program and exporting it as a graphic, or present the graphs/charts on a separate handout for your audience.

o In the **Task Pane (Slide Layout)**, select a Title & Chart slide layout (Tool tip says: "Title & Chart"). Use the drop-down menu to select the **Insert New Slide** option.
o Double-click on the chart placeholder. A 'Datasheet' window will appear. This is very similar to an Excel spreadsheet. Experiment with changing some of the headers and values in the datasheet. When you are finished, click the X to close the datasheet window.
o To modify colors, typefaces, axis labels or other parts of the chart, select **Chart>Chart Options** from the menu.

E. Blank Slide (Get creative)

o In the **Task Pane (Slide Layout)**, select a Blank slide layout (Tool tip says: "Blank"). Use the drop-down menu to select the **Insert New Slide** option.
o Insert the following text: [Using the Drawing Toolbar] (Hint: Use the Text Box tool. Select it, then click anywhere on your slide to begin typing text.)
   o Change the font to **ARIAL** and the size to **36pt**. Center the text.
o Using the **rectangle** and **oval** tools, draw four shapes on the left-hand side of your slide.
   o Using the **Fill Color** icon, change the color of your first shape to **red**. (NOTE: Before you can alter a shape or other object, you must be sure to select it by clicking **once** on the object.)
   o Using the **Shadow Style** icon, add a shadow to your second shape.
o Using the **line** and **arrow** tools, draw two parallel lines and two perpendicular arrows.
   o Using the **Line Color** icon, change the color of one of your lines to purple.
   o Increase that line's thickness by selecting a size using the **Line Style** icon.
   o Change one of your arrows to a double-headed one by selecting it and selecting an option using the **Arrow Style** icon.
o Experiment with some of the **AutoShapes** available to you from the Drawing toolbar.
o Press **CTRL+S** to save your work.

F. Ending Slide

The "Ending Slide" is a nice way to put a "finishing touch" on your presentation.

o In the **Task Pane (Slide Layout)**, select a Blank slide layout (Tool tip says: "Blank"). Use the drop-down menu to select the **Insert New Slide** option.
o Using a text box, enter an "ending" for your presentation. Most people put something like "Any Questions?" or "For More Information." Use a large font size such as 36 or 44pt, and experiment with the text color by using the **Font Color** icon.
o Below your ending, enter your name and contact information using a textbox. Use a smaller font size like 24 or 28pt.
   If you have time, insert a picture that represents the subject of your presentation. Be sure all of your elements are laid out in a pleasing and effective manner.

Activity 3 – Design Templates

Now that you have a working presentation, you can add some life and pizzazz to it by using some of the built-in templates available in PowerPoint. These are a collection of background and text colors, transitions, animations, font styles, etc. that fit together as a theme.

o Change to **Slide Sorter** view by selecting **View>Slide Sorter** from the main menu.
o In the **Task Pane (Slide Design)**, scroll down and view the available design templates for your presentations.
o Spend a few minutes applying different design templates to your presentation by clicking on the preview image.
o You can also access the **Slide Design** command anytime by right-clicking when the pointer is on a slide.

Note that you can also modify a design template further by changing its color scheme.

o After applying a design template, click **Color Schemes** from the **Task Pane (Slide Design)**.
o Select a color scheme to further modify your presentation.

Additional templates are available free of charge from the Microsoft Office website. Once you download a template, use the **Browse...** link at the bottom of the **Task Pane (Slide Design)** to open it.

To modify design templates, you can make changes to the template's **Slide Master**. A Slide Master consists of a Title Master and a Slide Master (for use with all other slides). For example, if you wanted a logo to appear on every slide after the title slide, you must place the logo on the Slide Master. Each time you create a new slide using this template, your logo or other text will appear.

o From the **View** menu, select **Master, then Slide Master**
o Select your Title Master from the list on the left. (Hint: If you're not sure which one is the Title Master, hover your mouse over the thumbnail images until a Tool Tip appears.)
o Click once in the box labeled "Click to edit Master title style."
o Change the font to something else. Click the close button on the pop-up menu to see your changes.
o Select your Slide Master and change the bullet color and style for first headings to a **red arrow** - Click anywhere in the line entitled "Click to edit Master text styles."
o Right-click and select "Bullets and Numbering" from the pop-up menu.
o Select the arrow graphic and change the color to red using the drop-down button next to "Color." Click the close button on the pop-up menu to return to Normal view.
o Navigate to your **Bulleted List** slide to see the changes you have made.

For more resources, visit http://gratisue.yahoo.com/lhilyer_lib/ .

Continued on next page

Other sources for handouts

You may have other documents (checklists, bibliographies, etc.) to distribute to the audience as supplementary material. Occasionally, you may also want provide copies of an article or other published material. Be sure to secure reprint permission with the copyright holder of the material or pay the appropriate copyright fees to the reproduction rights organization (RRO) in your country. (The Copyright Clearance Center (*http://www.copyright.com*) serves as the RRO for the United States.)

When to use handouts

Generally, handouts that are considered a summary of, or supplemental to, the original presentation should be given out at the end, *after* you have finished speaking. Audiences who have the handout in hand will often turn to it instead of listening to you.

For more complex presentations, or for presentations including hands-on activities, you may need to distribute the handouts beforehand or at the appropriate time during the live presentation. This approach is especially recommended when you are discussing statistical data. As mentioned in Chapter 7, large amounts of tabular data should not be dumped into a presentation slide. Use a graph summarizing the results on the displayed slide, then provide the supporting data tables as a separate handout. Because of the limitations of working memory, audience members cannot be expected to draw all of the necessary conclusions from a massive data table displayed on a slide for 30 seconds. They need time to examine the data and build their mental models of the content. Providing this information on paper makes the analysis easier for the audience member.

Encouraging useful note-taking

Many of the members of your audience attend presentations with their notebooks or journals at the ready. Note-taking can help some audience members to better process inform-ation, but can also increase the risk of cognitive overload. To encourage effective note-taking behaviour and effortful processing of your content, you can consider distributing an *advance organizer* handout before you begin. An advance organizer is a document that provides the outline for a topic but is missing some facts and concepts. Audience members must actively attend to the presentation content in order to be able to 'fill in' the blanks of the advance organizer to complete the outline. This active processing helps audience members to build stronger mental models of the content and can be especially useful in instructional situations where the audience will be tested on the material presented.

Summary

In summary, do not underestimate the learning potential of your handouts. Rather than treat them as a nuisance or an afterthought, think of them as your opportunity to more deeply connect with your audience and to provide them with additional rich resources they can use later, long after your short presentation is over. In Chapter 9, you will bring your effective handouts together with your polished script and slides to create a coherent and focused presentation experience for your audience.

Suggested further reading

Kinchin, I. (2006) 'Developing PowerPoint handouts to support meaningful learning', *British Journal of Educational Technology*, 37 (4): 647–50.

Krieger, S. (2005) *Microsoft Office Document Designer: Your Easy-to-Use Toolkit and Complete How-to Source for Professional-Quality Documents*. Redmond, WA: Microsoft Press.

Tufte, E.R. (2003) *The Cognitive Style of PowerPoint*, 2nd edn. Cheshire, CT: Graphics Press LLC.

White, J.V. (2005) 'Building blocks of functional design', *Technical Communication*, 52 (1): 37–41.

9

Integrating your script, slides and handouts through practice and rehearsal

At this point in the presentation creation process, you are ready to begin practising the delivery of your presentation. You have written an extensive report on your content, which you have used as the foundation for your presentation and from which you have identified the key content points that you have represented visually. What you are going to do now is to tightly integrate your spoken content, your visuals and your handouts into an effective presentation experience through an iterative process of rehearsal and editing.

Let me illustrate this for you through a scenario I personally experienced for a recent presentation assignment.

Vignette

As the chair of a library strategic planning committee, I was asked to deliver a short presentation on the planning processes we used and our progress to date on a number of initiatives. The audience for the presentation was our library's advisory committee, consisting of faculty, staff and student representatives who provide feedback on and input into the operation of the library. The time allotted was 15 minutes, with an additional 5–10 minutes for questions.

I realized early on that this presentation could easily be extended to an hour or more, as our library utilized a novel strategic planning process resulting in a non-traditional strategic planning document. As the implementation of related projects had been underway for nearly a year when I was asked to give the presentation, we also had considerable progress to report.

After some initial brainstorming and note-taking, I commenced writing a full summary report on our planning process and our progress so far. It ran to three pages and was written 'for publication'; that is, I treated the report, even though it was for internal use, as something that would ultimately be published. Approaching content in this way helped me to ensure a high-quality document from which I could derive my spoken remarks and my visuals.

After several early drafts, I completed a final draft and printed it out. I then reread the document and identified my 3–5 key points, my major content areas, and noted in the margin where I might visually represent some of this written content. From these notes, I next began creating the storyboards for my presentation.

After completing my storyboards, I at last began to work inside PowerPoint, turning them into rough slides. Once I completed my draft slides, I then returned to my written document. I opened the file in my word processor and then began to switch back and forth between programs, cutting and pasting sections of my document into the notes fields of my slides, performing a rough initial integration of written content with the corresponding visuals.

During early rehearsals, I often stopped to indicate in my notes when I needed to advance to the next slide. I used the technique recommended by Gene Zelazny in his book, Say It with Presentations (2006). He recommends you speak a sentence or two about the next slide before advancing to it. This primes the audience for what they are about to see and helps orient them to the information on the slide. Included in my overall timings were the brief pauses I took when a new slide was displayed on the screen to allow the audience time to comprehend the slide as a whole.

I then performed a full, untimed rehearsal of the presentation, where I could test the relationships between my spoken content and my visuals and begin to solidify the pacing of my presentation. As I worked through each slide, I reviewed the related written content, editing it down to its key ideas and generally pruning the written content so that it functioned mainly as talking points for me (though I did keep a few good phrases verbatim from the original document). I rehearsed the presentation two more times, each time adjusting visuals and/or their related written content until I was ready to begin timing my practices.

Next, I began to time myself while rehearsing. My allotted time period was 15 minutes, yet even after additional 'pruning' of the content, my first timed practice required 27 minutes to deliver the entire presentation. I had to go back and cut more material and try again. The next two times were 20 and 16 minutes. After some agonizing choices about what more to remove, the next practice time was 13 minutes, giving me a two-minute cushion for additional questions. The editing process involved not only eliminating spoken text, but also required editing of existing slides and the deletion of others.

I practised one additional time (14 minutes) to get an approximate duration, and then decided I was ready. I added a slide transition between all of my slides and spent an additional few hours doing some font formatting and *adjusting colours. Total time spent from start to finish: 18 hours (for a 15-minute presentation).*

When I delivered the presentation, for the most part it was a success. As a speaker, I struggle with my tendency to get more long-winded during an actual presentation, but this time I managed to conclude my presentation in 13 minutes. One concept, however, troubled the audience, and I spent extra time during the question and answer period clarifying what I had said during the presentation about that concept. This was something that I did not foresee during practice, but because I had extra time, I was able to use additional examples to more clearly explain myself. As I will be presenting this same presentation in the future to various audiences, I will need to further edit my script to clarify that particular point in the future and hopefully avoid any confusion on it.

My personal vignette above illustrates the iterative nature of the presentation process: successive rehearsals of your presentation are instrumental in setting proper pacing and timing and helping you bring your most important points into sharp focus for the audience. Also, each time you practise the material you become more comfortable with it. Being comfortable with what you are going to say contributes to a smooth and professional presentation.

Summary

Even after many years of giving presentations and after nearly five years teaching presentation skills, I still find that practice is the number one determinant of my success and that it requires more time now than it did when I was a novice presenter. I know from personal experience the confidence that comes with extensive practice, and that confidence enables me to be a better presenter. You too will benefit from rehearsal with your content – be sure to allow time for it.

10

Delivering a successful presentation

Now that you have extensively prepared and practised thoroughly, it is time to get your materials together, get to your venue and deliver that effective presentation!

This chapter will provide you with some recommendations and techniques you can use to more effectively present to your audience. This chapter also details some final preparations for a smooth presentation that you can complete before you step up to the podium. We will conclude with some strategies for handling common problems that might arise.

Before you leave the office ...

Prevent a presentation problem before it starts by following the steps below to properly back up your files and get your stuff together:

1. Review all of your presentation components (script, slides and handouts) *one final time.*

2. Store all of your resources (images, media clips, presentation file, etc.) together in *one* folder.

3. Save a copy of your presentation file (PowerPoint, Keynote and Impress) in 'Show' format.

4. Print and collate your handouts.

5. Pack any necessary equipment.

Review your materials one final time

The best time to find an error or fix a problem is *before* you leave for your conference or class. Double check your slides, your notes and your handouts to be sure everything is fine. In any case, it never hurts to have someone you trust review your materials for you; sometimes a fresh pair of eyes can spot errors you missed.

Gather all of your resources together in one folder

Make sure you have copies of your presentation file, any document files you need, the image files you used and especially any audio or video files that you plan to use stored in a *single folder* on your computer. PowerPoint, for example, only *links* to large multimedia files (audio/video), so if you have the PowerPoint file but forget the related media file, you will break the link and not be able to play it.

Note: *It is not necessary to take copies of your image files with you, as PowerPoint and most other software programs embed images directly into the presentation file.*

Once you have organized all of your files in one folder, copy that folder to a USB storage device or burn the folder onto a CD or DVD. For additional peace of mind, you can also copy the folder's contents to an online storage service such as Yahoo! Briefcase. Another option is to 'compress' the folder (using a compression utility such as WinZip) and e-mail the compressed file to yourself (if it does not exceed your e-mail provider's transfer limit).

Save your presentation in 'Show' format

Both PowerPoint and Keynote allow you to save a file in 'Show' format, so that when the file is opened it starts immediately in slide show mode. Unfortunately, Star Office/OpenOffice Impress does not allow you to save a file in 'Show' format, but if your presentation has no animation, you can export from Impress directly to a PDF, which can be edited to open in 'full-screen' mode just as a show would.

The advantage of starting in full-screen slide show mode is that it lets you begin right away, without delay. I once attended a conference where every speaker struggled for 30–45 seconds to locate the command to begin their slide show. As the seconds ticked away, they lost the attention of more and more audience members.

If you are the only presenter, or can arrange it with the conference organizer, start the show before the audience enters. For more dramatic effect, start the show but use the Darken Screen command (press the [B] key on the keyboard) to darken the screen. Once you stand up to begin, you can bring back the slide show (press the [B] key again) and begin speaking immediately, wasting no time.

Print off and collate your handouts

You would be surprised (or perhaps not) at how many presenters leave this step until the very last minute.

Conference organizers may request electronic or paper copies of your handouts beforehand, but if not, be sure to print your own and take them with you. As mentioned above, it is probably a good idea to take backup copies of your handout files in case you need to quickly print additional copies.

Pack any necessary equipment

Gather your laptop computer, LCD projector and any other equipment you need. Consider taking them along even if conference organizers will provide them. This ensures you can quickly switch to your own equipment if the equipment at the hotel or convention centre where you are speaking should fail.

Disaster planning

It is inevitable that at some point during your career as a presenter you will encounter a problem that seriously interferes with your presentation. Even if you worked for hours and have the most exquisite slides, you need to be prepared to stand and speak alone if necessary. It is worthwhile to brainstorm ahead of time what you might do if things go wrong and have contingency plans ready. Above all else, do not panic; the audience wants you to succeed as much as you do.

Probably the most common problems encountered by presenters have to do with technology failures (blown projector bulbs, malfunctioning computers, problems with the public address system, etc.). If the problem can be fixed by you (or someone else) in *less than one minute*, apologize to your audience and fix the problem. If the problem will take more than sixty seconds, you have several options you can use (while you wait for someone else to fix the problem):

- **Option 1.** Go 'retro' – use a whiteboard/chalkboard to add visuals to your lecture. (Carry a few whiteboard markers and some chalk in your briefcase for emergencies.)

- **Option 2.** Distribute your summary handout early and then guide the audience through the handout. *Do not* read long passages of this document; paraphrase and summarize as you move through it, remembering to emphasize your key points as you encounter them.

- **Option 3.** Break the audience into small groups and have them participate in a group activity (an 'icebreaker' exercise to get to know one another, or an activity related to your presentation content).

For options 1 and 2, it is probably best to continue your presentation without technology to avoid any unnecessary interruption to the flow of the presentation. You can always collect e-mail addresses and send presentation materials later or post them on a website for the audience to view at their leisure. The third option is useful when you *really must* wait the 5–10 minutes for the problem to be solved.

Delivering your presentation

This is the moment you (and your audience) have been waiting for – all of your preparations and practice have culminated in this opportunity for you to engage in meaningful, face-to-face communication with your audience. It is perfectly fine for you to be nervous – speaking in front of a large group of people can be intimidating. However, you should remember that you are well-prepared and have a mastery of your content that will help you as you present.

Meeting basic needs

The temperature and lighting of the room, the location of the bathrooms and when the snacks will arrive are all legitimate concerns of your audience members. These concerns can distract your audience from your presentation. Attempting to address them before you begin can help ensure a more pleasant experience for your audience.

Additionally, I often begin by asking my audience to set their cell phones to vibrate or silent mode. There is nothing more distracting than a cell phone ringing in a quiet auditorium. Some professors I work with require any student whose cell phone rings during class to stand up and sing a song, do a dance or recite a poem on the spot. While it might not be appropriate during a conference presentation, it might be worth a try when delivering library instruction.

Signalling

While practising your presentation, you coordinated verbal information (your script) with visual information (your slides) to balance the cognitive load among the two channels of working memory and to reduce the potential for cognitive overload. During a live presentation, one of the most effective instructional techniques you can employ is to 'signal' the importance of particular content to your audience at the appropriate time.

A 'signal' is an explicit or overt instruction to the audience that the following/preceding content is important. Some examples of verbal signalling include:

- 'Let me point out X to you.'
- 'This is the key theory supporting my hypothesis.'
- 'If you remember nothing else, remember ...'
- 'This will be on the test.'

As described in Chapter 1, for content to be learned, a learner must actively pay attention to it. Since the audience's full attention will wax and wane during your presentation, consciously and explicitly signalling important content helps direct the audience's attention to that content. Signalling can also be accomplished visually by physically pointing at some area of the slide displayed, or through the use of visual indicators such as arrows or checkmarks in diagrams or on images. As with repetition, you may feel awkward when first attempting conscious signalling. However, rest assured that you are actually helping the audience to understand and learn your content by directing their attention to its most important components.

Making eye contact

Eye contact with the audience is important. When you first begin speaking, make eye contact with a friendly face in the audience. As you progress through your presentation, make eye contact with others in different locations in the room. If you are using notes, remember to look up from them often to maintain a 'connection' with the audience.

Eye contact is difficult for some people, due to shyness, cultural values or other factors. One way to reduce your level of discomfort with making eye contact is to get acquainted with some of the audience members before the presentation starts. There are always 'early birds' to a conference session; try and be prepared 5–10 minutes *before* your scheduled presentation time to allow yourself time to introduce yourself and talk with the early arrivals. Making personal connections with a few audience members can be enough to put you at ease.

Pacing

Speaking too fast is one of the main complaints about presenters and is a function of how rigorously the content has been edited (or not). The feeling of 'too much content, too little time' can cause you to speak too quickly. Slow down your rate of speech, and pause briefly (one to two seconds) when displaying new visuals to allow the audience time to comprehend them.

No matter how little time you have in total, be sure to leave room to reiterate your key points (and redisplay your key points slide) near the end of your presentation. Repeating yourself may feel awkward, but repetition is a key method of elaboration, a process that will assist your audience to more richly encode your presented information and store it in their long-term memories.

Avoid distracting behaviours

One of the things I do most often is gesticulate wildly when I present; I enjoy the interaction with the audience and am excited about the content I am sharing. Wild gesticulation is often useful when engaging students, but it can be a distraction for other audiences. Another distracting behaviour is the repeated use of 'umm', 'uhh' and 'like' in your speech. Thorough practice with your content will help to eliminate this behaviour, as will slowing down your rate of speech.

Dress for success

No matter how casual your profession might be, I personally recommend that presenters dress more formally than their audience. Your professional appearance provides you with additional perceived credibility with the audience and can help boost your confidence. If you are presenting after food has been served, take a moment to check for any stray crumbs or stains, and also check your teeth for any remaining bits of spinach that might be glaringly visible.

Stay within the time limit

Be sure to stay within the time limit by making arrangements to see a clock, use a timer or have someone in the audience signal you at different intervals (e.g. ten minutes and five minutes before your time is up). There are also presentation remotes you can purchase that have built-in timers to help keep you on track. Ending your presentation on time shows your respect for the audience and for the speakers who follow. You can be sure that you will end your presentation within the time limit and still accomplish your goals by extensively practising your presentation beforehand as advocated in Chapter 9.

Where should I stand?

When possible, presenters should stand to the *left* of any visuals (screen, whiteboard, flip chart, etc.). As the audience 'reads' the presentation environment, they will start with you first and then move to any visuals displayed. This does not mean that you should stand perfectly still during the entire presentation. Feel free to move around the stage slowly or to step toward the screen and point out something on one of your slides.

Note: Avoid *using a laser pointer during your presentation as it can be a distraction. I prefer using an inexpensive telescoping metal pointer if I will need to point out any relevant features of the images or diagrams displayed.*

Should you want to really emphasize a particular point or redirect the audience's attention toward you, there are two easy techniques you can use: one is to use the [B] key during a slideshow (as mentioned above) to darken the screen momentarily. Another technique is to move to the 'position of power' which is *front-centre* of the stage. Inevitably, the audience's attention will quickly refocus on you.

Slide show controls

The three most popular slide presentation software programs all offer the capability to display your visuals in a slide show format. In addition to starting the show via a menu command or clicking an icon, they all permit you to control the slide show operation via keyboard shortcuts. If the presenters described earlier (who hunted vainly for the small *Slide Show* icon) had just pressed the [F5] key on their keyboard, their show would have started immediately. Use of keyboard shortcuts and other features of your software program's slide show mode can dramatically increase the professional 'polish' of your presentation delivery. *For more information on slide show controls, see Appendices A–C.*

Managing questions

Depending on your personal presentation style and level of comfort, you may want to field questions *during* your presentation or you may wish to wait until the end. To ensure that you return to any questions asked during the presentation, use the 'bin' or 'parking lot' method. Questions asked by your audience should be written down, either on a whiteboard or on a flip chart in the room. You can also ask a member of the audience to help you by keeping a list of questions asked. When you are ready for questions, you should address questions in the 'bin' first, and then open the floor for any new questions.

If you cannot answer a question right away, either because you do not have the appropriate data or truly do not know the answer, be honest. Ask for the questioner's contact information and indicate that you will follow up directly with them when you have an answer. Be sure to deliver on your promise by promptly providing them with an answer. If the answer is relevant to your entire audience, consider posting it on your website or otherwise making it widely available.

Concluding your presentation

When the question-and-answer period has concluded, if possible, give your audience a 15–20 second summary of your content or display your key points slide again as you thank them and receive your applause for an effective and well-received presentation. Distribute any supplemental handouts and your evaluation forms. Ask the audience to complete them immediately if there is time. If not, consider creating a web version that your audience can complete later.

Summary

Delivering an effective presentation takes preparation, hard work and a willingness to have a meaningful conversation with the audience about a topic that is important to you and to them. It takes practice to master the many techniques described above, but when used consistently and correctly, they can turn a hum-drum presentation into a genuine learning experience. If you are a novice presenter, do not attempt to utilize every technique during your next presentation. Try the ones that are the most appealing and assess their effectiveness for you. Incorporate the ones that work for you into your own practice, and then try a few more. Eventually, you will develop your own presentation style, incorporating the methods and techniques that work best for you and the audiences to whom you present. But just because you delivered your knockout presentation does not mean your work is done: the fourth step of the presentation process is reviewing your performance and evaluating your effectiveness, which we will address in the next chapter.

Suggested further reading

Alley, M. (2003) *The Craft of Scientific Presentations: Critical Steps to Succeed and Critical Errors to Avoid.* New York: Springer.

Anholt, R.R.H. (2006) *Dazzle 'Em with Style: The Art of Oral Scientific Presentation*, 2nd edn. Philadelphia: Elsevier Academic Press.

11

Evaluation for improvement

Review of your performance and the learning outcomes of your presentation is the fourth stage of the presentation process model first presented in Chapter 4 and is essential to continuous improvement of your skills as a presenter. Review provides you with internal and external feedback for improvement, and gives you some assurance that your audience comprehends your content, is retaining it, and will be able to use it again in later situations.

Types of evaluation

Instructional analysis differentiates between two types of evaluation (or assessment): *formative* and *summative*. While preparing your presentation, *formative* evaluation is done as part of the practice and rehearsal stage. Your presentation is constantly being shaped with each successive practice and rehearsal. Formative evaluation can also be external, such as the feedback you receive from individuals who are observing your rehearsal or from videotaping or audiotaping yourself as you practise.

Summative evaluation is completed after a presentation has been delivered, either before participants leave the room or sometimes after as part of an overall conference or workshop evaluation. In addition to the conference or workshop evaluation, consider setting aside time to develop and administer your own evaluation form. The obvious advantage to creating your own assessment instrument is the freedom you have in which questions you ask. A superb set of questions to use for summative evaluation can be found in Andy Goodman's book *Why Bad Presentations Happen to Good Causes: And How to Ensure They Won't Happen to Yours* (2006: 78). Suggested questions are included for different categories such as the clarity of the presentation, the amount of audience interaction with the presenter and the quality of visuals used.

Structured self-reflection can also be an excellent form of summative evaluation. Thinking about where you succeeded and where you stumbled can provide a picture of your strengths as a presenter as well as areas of performance that need improvement. Consider not only your own performance as a speaker but also the impact of your visuals and the quality of your handouts. Try videotaping yourself the next time you present in front of a live audience. This will give you a visual record of how you present and can be helpful for spotting distracting behaviours to reduce or eliminate from your performance.

Assessing learning

It is often difficult to assess learning outcomes, especially from short, one-time presentations. Lengthier instructional presentations or workshops better lend themselves to conducting a learning assessment. One alternative to a full assessment plan is to conduct a follow-up survey or request completion of a short quiz by attendees to your presentation. Survey response rates are usually low, so you would need to consider that when evaluating any results, but the information obtained is often beneficial and can highlight areas for improvement. Quizzes should be short (5–10 questions) and consist of simple test items (true/false, multiple choice, etc.). There are multiple websites and software programs (both free and paid) for quiz creation and administration.

Summary

No matter what type of assessments you conduct, simply gathering data and not analysing it does not help you improve your performance. Use your data to focus your efforts on areas of improvement: if your audience indicates you moved too fast through the material, concentrate more on pacing when you practise. If you felt rushed because you did not have enough time to complete your material, consider a more rigorous editing process during the preparation phase, or adjust your timing during the practice phase. If your assessments of audience learning indicate some content points were poorly understood, make changes to your presentation components (script/slides/handouts) to incorporate clearer examples or better illustrate the important concepts.

Appendices

Appendix A
Using Microsoft PowerPoint 2007

PowerPoint 2007 is part of the Microsoft Office 2007 suite of programs and is designed for the creation of presentation slides. Below is a short, hands-on introduction to the program for new users or for those who need a refresher. This appendix is also useful for users familiar with PowerPoint 2003 and who want an introduction to the new interface in the 2007 version.

Contents

- *Starting PowerPoint 2007*
- *Program layout*
- *Placeholders*
- *Slide layouts*
- *Inserting new slide objects*
- *Saving your file*
- *Adding and formatting text*
- *Inserting images*
- *Inserting clip art*
- *Using the drawing toolbar*

- *Using slide themes*
- *Using the Notes pane*
- *Adding slide transitions*
- *Playing a slide show*
- *Saving your presentation in 'Show' format*
- *Suggested resources*

Starting PowerPoint

To launch PowerPoint: **Start > All Programs > Microsoft Office > PowerPoint 2007.**

Program layout

At the top is the **Office 'jewel'** (see Figure A.1). Click on it to access traditional file menu operations such as saving and printing your document.

Next is the **'Ribbon'** interface. New to all Microsoft Office 2007 programs is the new 'Ribbon' interface, which takes the place of many drop-down menus in previous versions.

On the *left* is the **Outline/Slides** pane, in the *middle* is the **Slide Workspace** and at the *bottom* is the **Notes** pane. The default slide design for a blank presentation as shown in Figure A.1 uses black text on a white background.

Figure A.1 **The PowerPoint 2007 program layout**

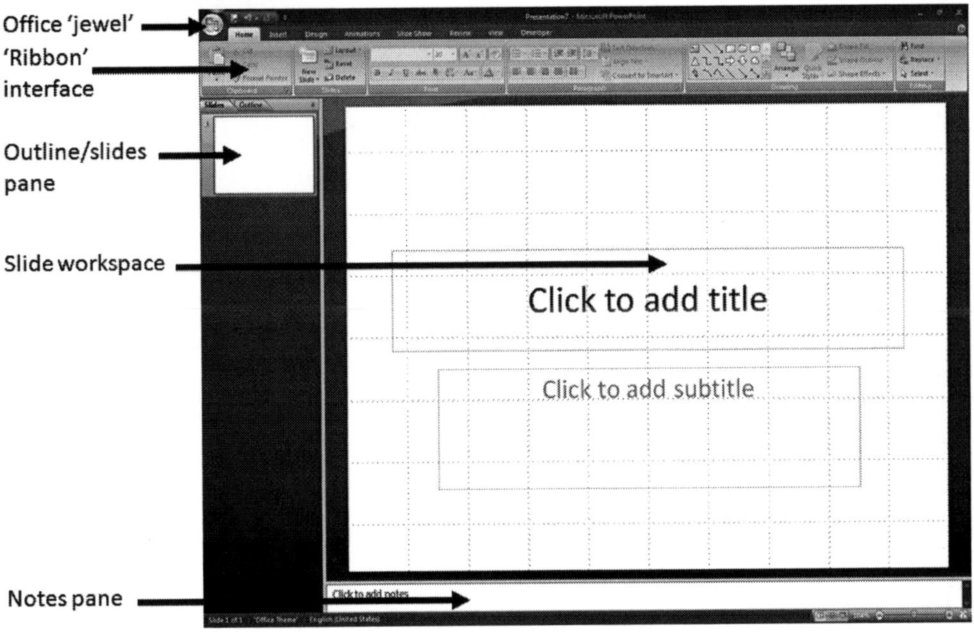
Office 'jewel'
'Ribbon' interface
Outline/slides pane
Slide workspace
Notes pane
Click to add title
Click to add subtitle
Click to add notes

Placeholders

Notice that the words 'Effective Presentations' are contained within a box denoted by a dashed line (see Figure A.2). These boxes are known as placeholders. PowerPoint uses specific placeholders to contain different types of objects. The two boxes above contain text, so they are known as text boxes.

Placeholders can also hold images, clip art, spreadsheets, charts and movie or sound clips. They can be resized and reshaped as needed to fit your content.

Figure A.2   Placeholders on a title slide layout

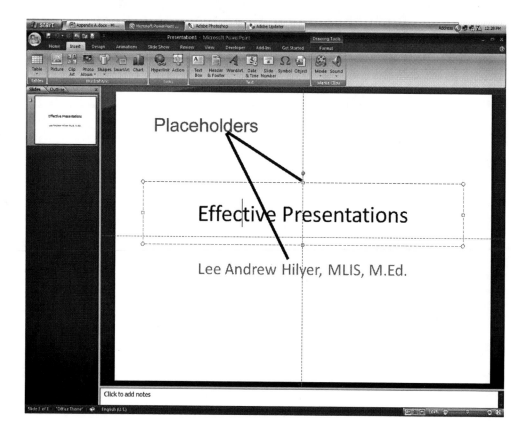

Slide layouts

PowerPoint combines multiple placeholders into a predetermined arrangement known as a *slide layout* (see Figure A.3). You can use one of these built-in layouts or create your own by inserting placeholders or objects (images, clip art, etc.) onto a blank slide.

The slide pictured above uses two placeholders: a text box for the title of the slide, and a text box for the presenter's name.

Figure A.3 Pre-defined slide layouts

Slide layouts

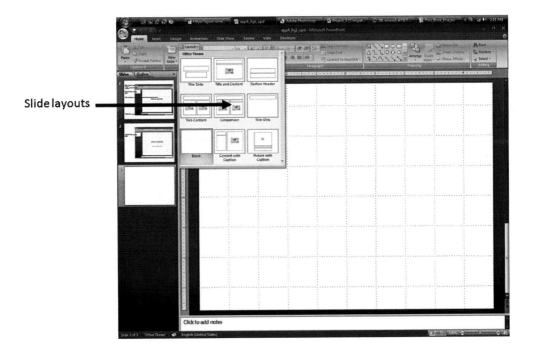

Inserting new slides

You can insert a new slide with a pre-defined slide layout (see Figure A.3) by clicking on the lower half of the *New Slide* icon.

Inserting new slide objects

You can also insert objects (photos and media clips) and placeholders (text boxes) at any time using the options on the **Insert** tab (see Figure A.4) or by the six icons in the centre of the placeholder (see Figure A.3).

Figure A.4 The Insert tab of the Ribbon

Placing text boxes

To place a new text box on a slide, click the *Text Box* icon on the **Insert** tab of the Ribbon.

Saving your file

In order to save your file, click the Office 'jewel' or press [ALT] + [F] on your keyboard to open the File menu (see Figure A.5).

Figure A.5 File and print options available by clicking the Office 'jewel'

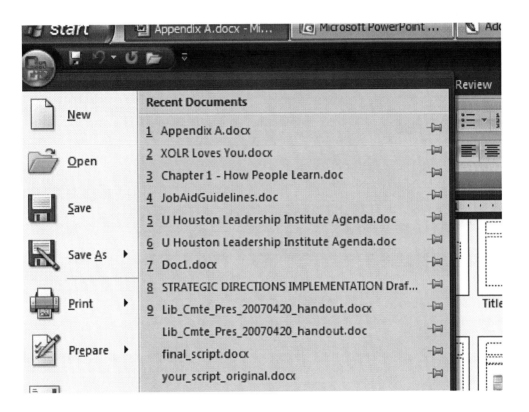

All programs in the Office 2007 suite use Microsoft's new XML-based file format. The new files use the extension **.pptx** and result in much smaller file sizes than previous versions of PowerPoint.

PowerPoint 2003 users can download the *Office 2007 Compatibility Pack* from Microsoft to be able to open and view files created in PowerPoint 2007.

You also have the option of saving the file in previous formats (.ppt) to be able to share them with people who do not have Office 2007.

Adding and formatting text

To add text to a slide, it must be contained within a text box (see Figure A.6). Click inside the text box to add your own text.

Figure A.6 Text boxes on a slide layout

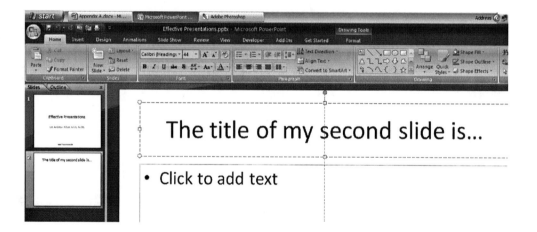

You can change the font type, size or colour via options in the **Home** tab (see Figure A.7). Be sure to *first* select the text you want to change, or, if you want to apply the changes to all the text in a text box, select the entire text box by clicking on its border.

Figure A.7 The Font menu in the Home tab

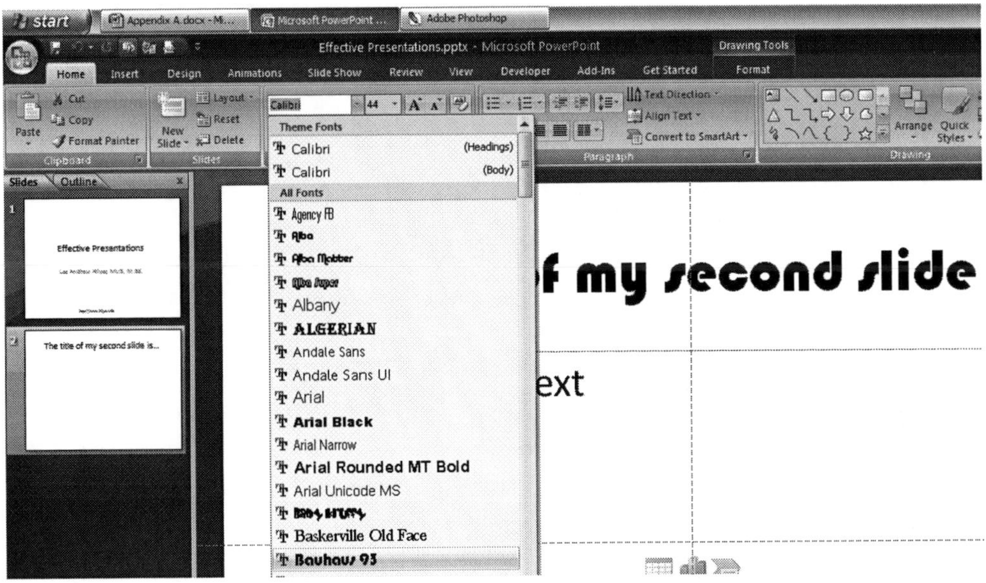

Inserting images

To place an image onto a slide, click the *Picture* icon on the
Insert tab. Browse to the location of the file you want to use,
and then click **[Insert]**. If you click the **Insert Picture** icon
from within the placeholder, the image will be placed inside
it (see Figure A.8). If not, your image may need to be resized
manually.

Figure A.8   The Insert Picture dialogue box

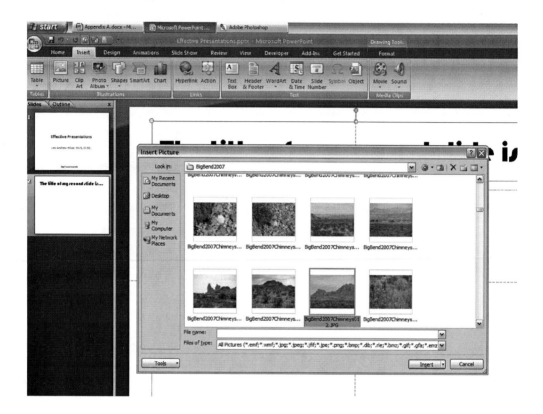

Framing your images

PowerPoint 2007 offers new and more elegant ways to frame your images, though be sure not to distract your audience with irrelevant decoration (see Figure A.9). Experiment with some of the new options, but be sure to use the same frame style throughout your presentation to maintain visual unity.

Figure A.9 Frame options for your images

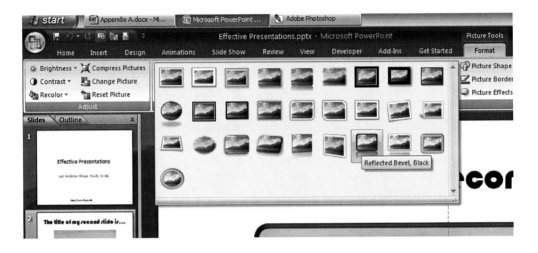

Inserting clip art

You can also insert clip art (drawings and illustrations) into your presentation (see Figure A.10). Microsoft has a library of free clip art you can download and use. There are also many free sources of clip art on the Web.

Since most clip art files are 'vector-based', they are drawn mathematically rather than pixel by pixel, and can be resized without any loss of quality.

To insert a piece of clip art, click the *Clip Art* icon on the **Insert** tab of the Ribbon.

Figure A.10   Clip art placed on a slide

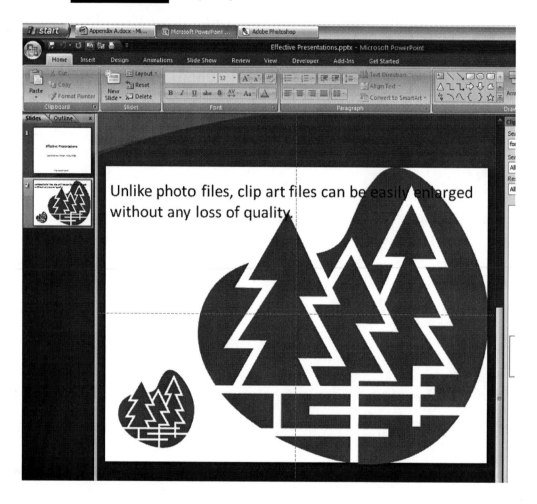

Using the drawing toolbar

In addition to inserting images and clip art, you can also use PowerPoint's built-in drawing tools to create your own objects for your slides (see Figure A.11).

Formatting options for shapes are greatly improved in

PowerPoint 2007 and can be accessed via the *Quick Styles* icon in the **Drawing** section of the **Home** tab.

To draw a shape on your slide, select the shape's icon from the palette, place your pointer on the slide, then click and drag to the desired size.

Figure A.11   Shapes and lines available from the drawing toolbar

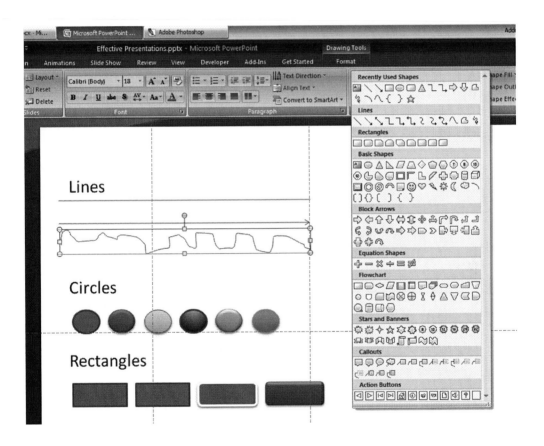

Using slide themes

In the new Office 2007, users can apply **themes** (formatting elements, colour choices, layout, etc.) to their documents and presentations (see Figure A.12). PowerPoint's live preview option lets you see immediately how your slides would look with a particular theme applied.

Many of these themes can be used across multiple Office programs (Word, Excel, etc.) so that your written handout can be formatted in Word using the same thematic elements as your presentation.

Themes help you achieve a consistent graphic identity across both your presentations and your written documents.

Figure A.12   'Prefab' slide theme applied to presentation

Using the Notes pane

Below the slide workspace is the Notes pane, where you can add notes or paste text from another document (see Figure A.13). You can then print handouts that include these notes, either for your own use as speaker notes or as a basis for your handout.

Figure A.13   The Notes pane

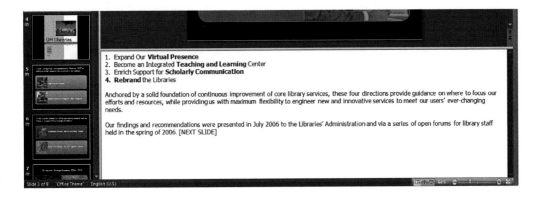

To preview notes pages, click the *Notes Pages* icon on the **View** tab (see Figure A.14).

Figure A.14   'Notes Pages' view of presentation

Adding slide transitions

Slide transitions are subtle effects that are played when 'transitioning' from one slide to the next (see Figure A.15). They should be applied to *all* slides in your presentation, and should be subtle (the 'wipe' and 'fade' options are the subtlest and least likely to distract your audience).

They should also be *fast* – you do not want to waste your precious time with the audience waiting on your special effects to finish.

Once you have selected a slide transition that you like,

click [**Apply to All**] and be sure to select **Fast** as the [Transition Speed].

Playing a slide show

Click the **Slide Show** tab in the ribbon to display your playback options (see Figure A.16).

To start a slide show, click the *From Beginning* icon at the far left of the tab. You can also simply press [**F5**] on your keyboard.

To advance to the next slide, click the left mouse button, or press [**Enter**], [**Space**] or the [→] (right-arrow) on your keyboard.

To darken the screen, press the [B] key on your keyboard. Press it again to return to the current slide. Try it also using [W].

To end your slide show, press the [Esc] key on your keyboard or right-click on the screen and select *End Show* from the pop-up menu.

You can also access a full list of slide show keyboard shortcuts by right-clicking on the screen with your mouse and selecting *Help* from the pop-up menu.

Saving your presentation in 'Show' format

As mentioned in Chapter 10, PowerPoint 2007 (and 2003) offers the option to save your presentation in 'Show' format, which means that when the file is next opened, it will *start* in slide show mode.

Note: *'Show' files cannot be edited. Only the original presentation file can be changed.*

To save your file in 'Show' format:

1. Click the Office 'jewel' or press [ALT] + [F] on your keyboard to open the File Menu.

2. Click **Save As,** and then click **PowerPoint Show.**

3. Select the location where you want to save the file, then click [Save]. The file extension for PowerPoint Show files is **.ppsx.**

You can also publish your presentation as a PDF file or save your file in the older (PowerPoint 97/2003) format.

Suggested resources

There are many excellent resources available both in print and online to help you learn to use PowerPoint 2007. Visit *http://office.microsoft.com* for training and tutorials on PowerPoint 2007. Below are a few additional resources for learning more.

Books

Bajaj, G. (2007) *Cutting Edge PowerPoint 2007® for Dummies®*. Indianapolis, IN: Wiley.

Rutledge, P.-A., Bajaj, G. and Mucciolo, T. (2007) *Special Edition Using Microsoft Office PowerPoint 2007*. Indianapolis, IN: Que.

These authors are well-known authorities on PowerPoint and these are two of the best new books on PowerPoint 2007.

Palaia, W. and Palaia, C. (2005) *Degunking Microsoft Office*. Scottsdale, AZ: Paraglyph Press.

The Palaias have written an excellent guide to making Microsoft Office programs work more efficiently for you. They recommend suggested changes to settings and program options that result in better performance from PowerPoint and other programs. Though written for Office 2003, many of the suggestions will be applicable to Office 2007 programs as well.

Appendix B
Using Apple Keynote Version 3

Keynote 3 is Apple's answer to PowerPoint and is available exclusively for Macintosh computers. It is available as part of the iWork software package. Below is a short, hands-on introduction to the program for new users or for those who need a refresher.

Contents

- *Starting Keynote 3*
- *Program layout*
- *Saving your file*
- *Placeholders*
- *Slide masters*
- *Adding and formatting text*
- *Inserting images*
- *Using shapes*
- *Using slide themes*
- *Using the Notes pane*
- *Adding slide transitions*
- *Playing a slide show*
- *Saving your presentation in 'Show' format*
- *Suggested resources*

Starting Keynote 3

To launch Keynote 3, double click the icon in your program dock. If you do not have the program icon in your dock, use the Finder to browse to your *iWork '06* folder, and then double-click the Keynote 3 icon.

Program layout

You are first requested to choose a theme for your presentation (see Figure B.1). The default is 'White' (black text on a white background). Click [**Choose**] to select it.

Across the top of the window is a toolbar with options (left to right) for inserting new slides, adding text and other objects, and formatting text and shapes.

Figure B.1   The Keynote 3 opening screen

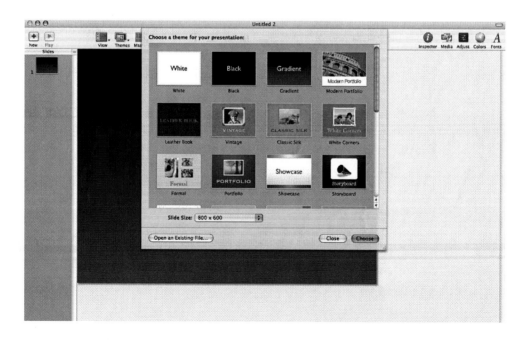

Saving your file

To save your file, select **Save** from the File menu (or press [CMD] + [S]).

Placeholders

Notice that the words 'Double-click to edit' are contained within a box (see Figure B.2). These boxes are known as placeholders. Keynote uses specific placeholders to contain different types of objects.

The two boxes above contain text, so they are known as text boxes. Placeholders can also hold images, clip art, spreadsheets, charts and movie or sound clips. They can be resized and reshaped as needed to fit your content.

To add a new text box to your slide, click the *Text* icon in the toolbar above the slide workspace.

Figure B.2   Placeholders on a title slide master

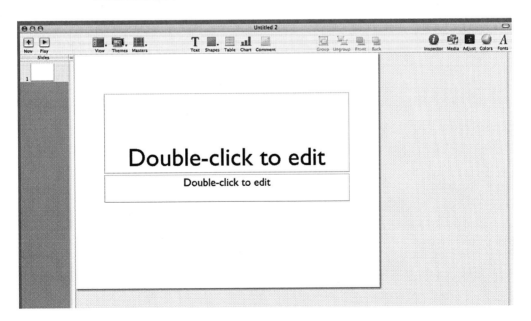

Slide masters

Keynote combines multiple placeholders into a predetermined arrangement known as a *slide master* (see Figure B.3). You can use one of these built-in masters to format your slide or create your own by inserting placeholders or objects (images, clip art, etc.) onto a blank slide.

The slide pictured above uses two placeholders: a text box for the title of the slide and a text box to hold a list of bullet points.

To insert a new slide, click the **New [+]** button at the top left of the window.

Figure B.3   **Pre-defined slide masters**

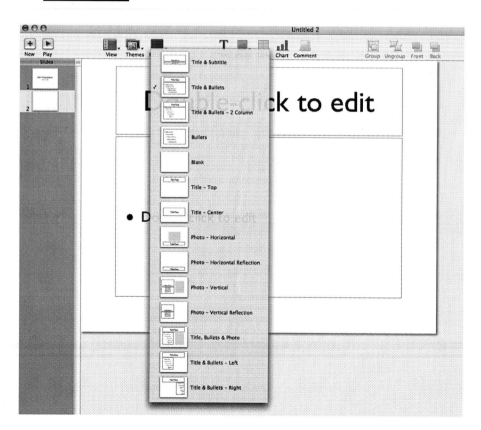

Adding and formatting text

To add text to a slide, it must be contained within a text box. Click inside the text box to add new text or to edit existing text.

You can change the font type, size or colour via options in the *Fonts* window (see Figure B.4). Be sure to *first* select the text you want to change, or, if you want to apply the changes to all text in a text box, select the entire text box by clicking on its border.

Figure B.4 Click the *Fonts* icon to access font formatting options

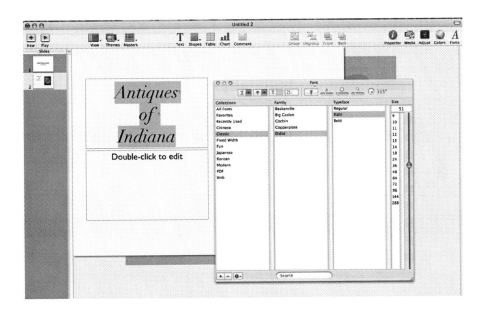

Inserting images

To place an image onto a slide, click the *Media* icon in the toolbar (see Figure B.5). Use the Media browser to navigate to the location of the file you want to use. Click and drag your photo from the Media browser window to your slide workspace.

You can adjust the size of your photograph by grabbing one of the selection handles on the image and dragging to resize.

Figure B.5   Insert a picture using the Media browser

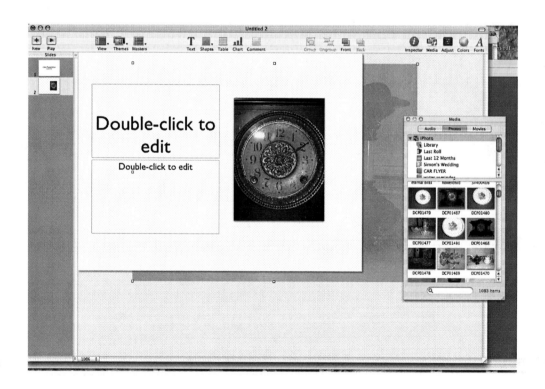

Using shapes

In addition to inserting images and other media, you can also use Keynote's built-in shape tools to create your own objects for your slides.

To draw a shape on your slide, select the shape's icon from the *Shapes* palette (see Figure B.6), place your pointer on the slide, then click and drag to the desired size.

To change the shape's colour or other formatting attributes, click once on the shape to select it, and then click the *Inspector* icon in the toolbar to access formatting options.

Figure B.6 The shapes toolbar and some shape examples

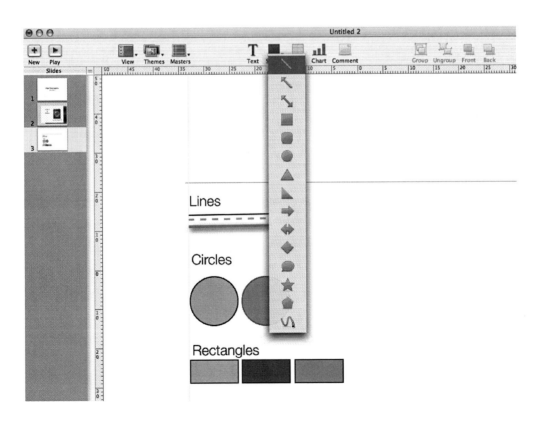

Using slide themes

In Keynote, users can apply *themes* (formatting elements, colour choices, slide layouts, etc.) to their presentations (see Figure B.7).

Themes help you achieve a consistent graphic identity across your presentation.

Figure B.7   The themes palette

Using the Notes pane

Below the slide workspace is the Notes pane, where you can add notes or paste text from another document (see Figure B.8). You can then print handouts that include these notes, either for your own use as speaker notes or as a basis for your handout.

Figure B.8   Notes pane

Antiquing in Indiana can be a pleasure. You can find treasures like this Seth Thomas Clock owned by the Millis family.

Adding slide transitions

Slide transitions are subtle effects that are played when 'transitioning' from one slide to the next (see Figure B.9). They should be applied to *all* slides in your presentation, and should be subtle. Any 'wipe' or 'fade' options are the subtlest and the least likely to distract your audience.

They should also be *fast*; you do not want to waste your precious time with the audience waiting on your special effects to finish.

To add slide transitions, click the *Inspector* icon then click the *Transitions* icon (second from left).

Once you have selected a slide transition that you like, click **[Apply to All]** and be sure to reduce the *Duration* to 0.5 to 1 second.

Figure B.9 Slide transition options

Playing a slide show

To access the slide show settings (see Figure B.10), click the *Inspector* icon, then click the *Document* icon (far left).

To start a slide show, from the **View** menu, click *Play Slideshow*, or press the *Play* icon in the toolbar. The keyboard shortcut is [OPT] + [CMD] + [P].

To advance to the next slide, click the left mouse button, or press [**Return**], [**Space**] or the [→] (right-arrow) on your keyboard.

To darken the screen, press the [B] key on your keyboard. Press it again to return to the current slide.

To end your slide show, press the [**Esc**] or [Q] keys on your keyboard.

Saving your presentation in 'Show' format

As mentioned in Chapter 10, Keynote offers the option to save your presentation in 'Show' format, which means that when the file is next opened, it will *start* in slide show mode.

Note: *'Show' files cannot be edited. Only the original presentation file can be changed.*

To save your file in 'Show' format:

1. Click the *Inspector* icon (or **View > Inspector**).
2. Select the checkbox labelled 'Automatically play upon open'.
3. Save your file.

You can also publish your presentation as a PDF file or

Figure B.10 Slide show settings

save your file in a format compatible with Microsoft PowerPoint.

Suggested resources

Apple Computer, Inc. (2006) *Keynote 3 User's Guide.* Cupertino, CA: Apple Computer.

Appendix C
Using OpenOffice Impress
Version 2.2

Impress is the slide presentation program found in the free, open source office suite known as OpenOffice. Impress is also available as part of the Sun StarOffice suite. Below is a short introduction to the program for new users or for those who need a refresher.

Note: *The screenshots used are from the StarOffice 7 version of Impress and are nearly identical to those found in OpenOffice Impress.*

Contents

- *Starting Impress*
- *Program layout*
- *Placeholders*
- *Slide layouts*
- *Inserting new slide objects*
- *Saving your file*
- *Adding and formatting text*
- *Inserting images*

- *Using the drawing toolbar*
- *Using slide designs*
- *Using the Notes pane*
- *Adding slide transitions*
- *Playing a slide show*
- *Saving your presentation in 'Show' format*
- *Suggested resources*

Starting Impress

To launch Impress, click **Start > All Programs > OpenOffice > Impress.**

Program layout

On the *left* is a **toolbar** containing some of the most-used features and in the *middle* is the **Slide Workspace.** Additional features can be accessed through the menus and the toolbars at the top (see Figure C.1).

Impress starts you in the *Drawing View*. To change your view options, click **View > Workspace.**

The default slide design for a blank presentation as shown in Figure C.1 uses black text on a white background.

Figure C.1 The Impress program layout (drawing view)

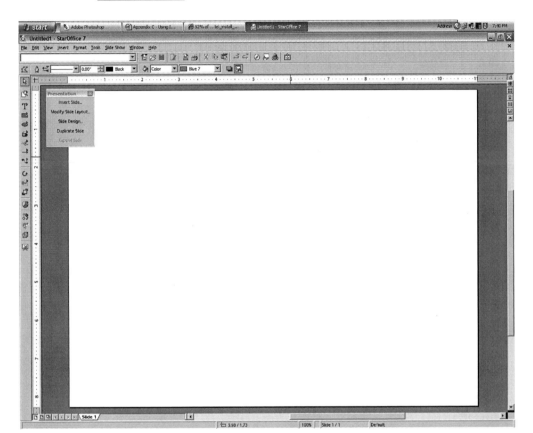

Placeholders

The words 'Click to add text' are contained within a box known as a placeholder (see Figure C.2). Impress uses specific placeholders to contain different types of objects. The two boxes above contain text, so they are known as text boxes.

Placeholders can also hold images, clip art, Excel spreadsheets, charts and movie or sound clips. They can be resized and reshaped as needed to fit your content.

Use the Text Box tool on the toolbar to insert a new text box.

Figure C.2 Placeholders on a title slide layout

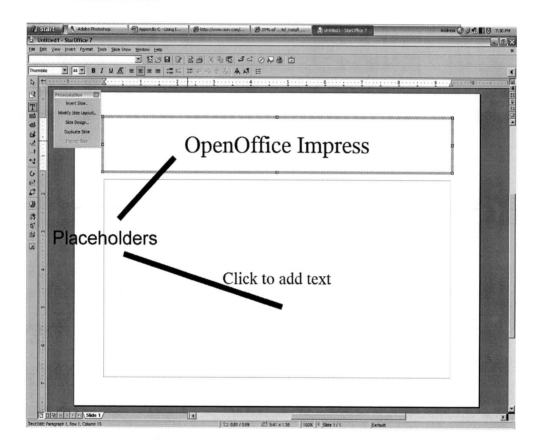

Slide layouts

Impress combines multiple placeholders into a pre-determined arrangement known as a *slide layout* (see Figure C.3). You can use one of these built-in layouts or create your own by inserting placeholders or objects (images, clip art, etc.) onto a blank slide.

Inserting new slides

You can insert a new slide with a pre-defined slide layout (see above) by clicking on **Insert > Slide**.

Modifying slide layouts

To modify a slide layout, click **Format > Modify Layout**.

Figure C.3   Pre-defined slide layouts

Inserting new slide objects

You can also insert additional slide objects (photos, charts, spreadsheets, etc.). Click the **Insert** menu, and then select an option from the list below (see Figure C.4).

Saving your file

To save your file, click **File > Save**.

In addition to the Impress native file format (.sxi for StarOffice, .odp for OpenOffice), you also have the option of saving the file in Microsoft PowerPoint format (.ppt).

Figure C.4   Use the Insert menu to add new slide objects

Adding and formatting text

To add text to a slide, it must be contained within a text box. Click inside the text box to add your own text (see Figure C.5).

Figure C.5   Text boxes on a slide layout

You can change the font type, size or colour via the toolbar above the slide workspace (see Figure C.6). Be sure to *first* select the text or entire textbox you want to change.

Figure C.6 **Toolbar formatting options**

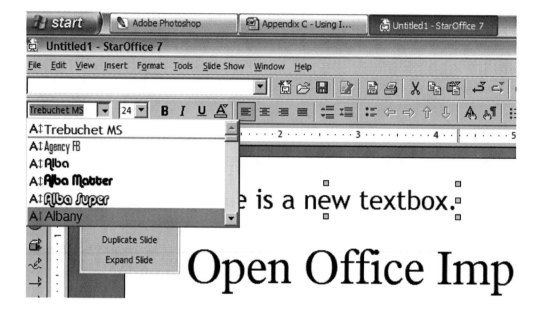

Inserting images

To place an image or piece of clip art onto a slide, click **Insert > Graphic** (see Figure C.7). Browse to the location of the file you want to use, and then click [**Open**].

As does PowerPoint, StarOffice Impress includes several hundred clip art and image files that can be used in your presentations. There are also many free sources of clip art on the Web.

Most clip art files are 'vector-based', meaning they are drawn mathematically rather than pixel by pixel, and can be resized without any loss of quality.

Figure C.7   The Insert Graphics dialogue box

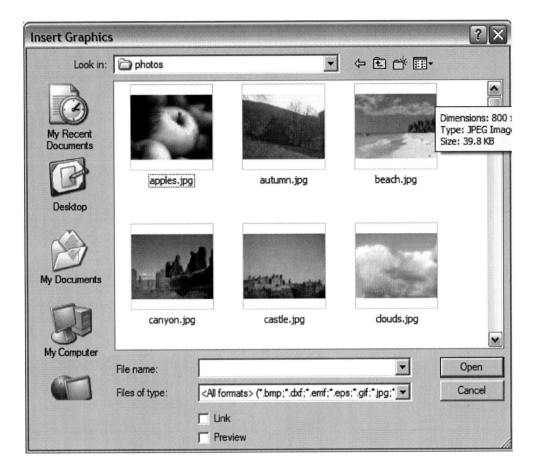

Using the drawing toolbar

In addition to inserting images and clip art, you can also use Impress's built-in drawing tools to draw your own shapes for your slides (see Figure C.8).

To draw a shape on your slide, select the shape's icon from the left toolbar, place your pointer on the slide, then click and drag to the desired size.

Figure C.8 Shapes and lines available from the drawing toolbar

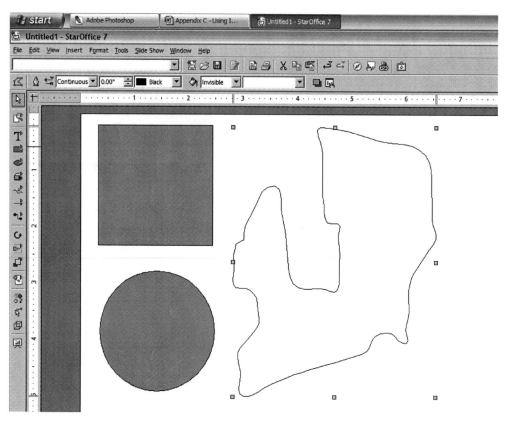

Using slide designs

To load a slide design, a coordinated set of formatting elements, colour choices, layout, etc., click **Format > Styles > Slide Design,** then click **[Load ...]** to load the slide designs (see Figure C.9) Scroll to *Presentation Backgrounds* then select one you like. Click the **[More >>]** button if the preview window is not visible.

Slide designs help you achieve a consistent graphic identity across all the slides in your presentation.

Figure C.9 Load slide designs when needed

Using the Notes View

To view your presentation in 'Notes View', click **View > Workspace > Notes View** (see Figure C.10).

Figure C.10 The Notes View

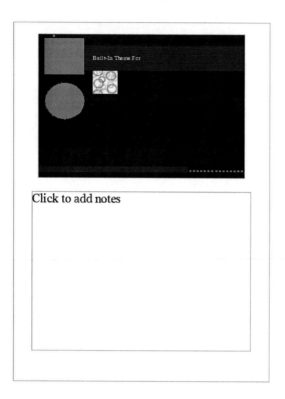

Click to add notes

Adding slide transitions

Slide transitions are subtle effects that are played when 'transitioning' from one slide to the next and should be applied to all slides in a presentation.

They should also be *fast* – you do not want to waste your precious time with the audience waiting on your special effects to finish.

Click **Slide Show** > **Slide Transition** for transition options (see Figure C.11).

Figure C.11   Slide transition options

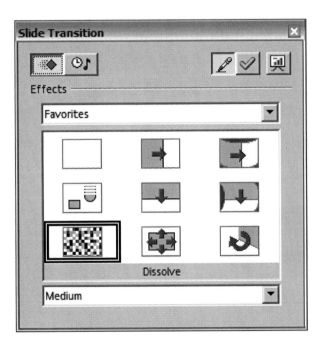

Running a slide show

To start a slide show, click the *Slide Show* menu item or press **[F9]** (see Figure C.12).

Figure C.12   Slide show controls

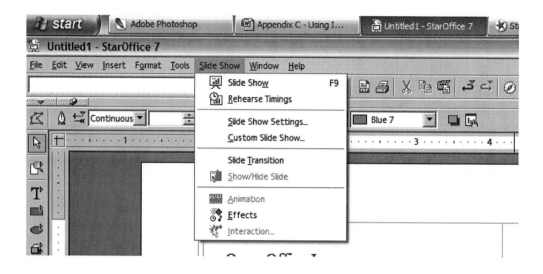

To advance to the next slide, click the left mouse button, or press [**Enter**], [**Space**] or the [→] (right-arrow) on your keyboard.

To darken the screen, press the [**B**] key on your keyboard. Press it again to return to the current slide. Try it also using [**W**].

To end your slide show, press the [**Esc**] key on your keyboard or right-click on the screen and select *End Show* from the pop-up menu.

Saving your presentation in 'Show' format

While Impress for StarOffice 7 does not allow you to save files in 'show' format, you can export your presentation to

Adobe PDF format. You can then use Adobe Reader to show the file in full-screen format.

While you do lose any individual slide object animations, slide transitions are usually transferred or can be easily added via the conversion options.

To save your file in PDF format:

1. From the **File** menu, select **Export to PDF**.

2. Name your file and select a save location.

3. Open the file with Adobe Reader.

4. Press [**CTRL**] + [**L**] to switch to full-screen mode.

Suggested resources

OpenOffice website: *http://www.openoffice.org/*

Download the free OpenOffice suite (including Impress) from this site. The site also provides help and support information.

StarOffice Website *http://www.sun.com/staroffice/*

Here you will find information on StarOffice version 8, including a downloadable trial version.

References

Alley, M. and Neeley, K.A. (2005) 'Rethinking the design of presentation slides: a case for sentence headlines and visual evidence', *Technical Communication*, 52 (4): 417–26.

Alley, M., Schreiber, M., Ramsdell, K. and Muffo, J. (2006) 'How the design of headlines in presentation slides affects audience retention', *Technical Communication*, 53 (2): 225–34.

Baddeley, A.D. (1998) *Human Memory: Theory and Practice*, rev. edn. Boston: Allyn & Bacon.

Chandler, P. and Sweller, J. (1991) 'Cognitive load theory and the format of instruction', *Cognition and Instruction*, 8 (4): 293–332.

Clark, R.C., Nguyen, F. and Sweller, J. (2006) *Efficiency in Learning: Evidence-Based Guidelines to Manage Cognitive Load*. San Francisco: Jossey-Bass.

Driscoll, M.P. (2005) *Psychology of Learning for Instruction*, 3rd edn. Boston: Pearson Allyn & Bacon.

Goodman, A. (2006) *Why Bad Presentations Happen to Good Causes*. Santa Monica, CA: Cause Communications.

Hamilton, R.J. and Ghatala, E.S. (1994) *Learning and Instruction*. New York: McGraw-Hill.

Lidwell, W., Holden, K. and Butler, J. (2003) *Universal Principles of Design*. Gloucester, MA: Rockport.

Mayer, R.E. (2001) *Multimedia Learning*. Cambridge and New York: Cambridge University Press.

Mayer, R.E. and Moreno, R. (2003) 'Nine ways to reduce cognitive load in multimedia learning', *Educational Psychologist*, 38 (1): 43–52.

Miller, G.A. (1956) 'The magical number seven, plus or minus two: some limits on our capacity for processing information', *Psychological Review*, 63: 81–97.

Paivio, A. (1986) *Mental Representations: A Dual Coding Approach*. Oxford: Oxford University Press.

Poole, A. (2005) 'Which are more legible: serif or sans-serif typefaces?' Retrieved 15 April 2007 from: *http://www. alexpoole.info/academic/literaturereview.html*.

Reigeluth, C.M. (1999) 'What is instructional-design theory and how is it changing?', in C.M. Reigeluth (ed.), *Instructional-Design Theories and Models Volume II: A New Paradigm of Instructional Theory*. Mahwah, NJ: Lawrence Erlbaum Associates, pp. 5–29.

Sweller, J. (1999) *Instructional Design in Technical Areas*. Melbourne: ACER.

Sweller, J. and Chandler, P. (1991) 'Evidence for cognitive load theory', *Cognition and Instruction*, 8 (4): 351–62.

Sweller, J. and Chandler, P. (1994) 'Why some material is difficult to learn', *Cognition and Instruction*, 12 (3): 185–233.

Sweller, J., van Merrienboer, J.J.G. and Paas, F.G.W.C. (1998) 'Cognitive architecture and instructional design', *Educational Psychology Review*, 10 (3): 251–96.

Sweller, J., Chandler, P., Tierney, P. and Cooper, M. (1990) 'Cognitive load as a factor in the structuring of technical material', *Journal of Experimental Psychology: General*, 119 (2): 176–92.

Tufte, E.R. (2001) *The Visual Display of Quantitative Information*, 2nd edn. Cheshire, CT: Graphics Press.

Tufte, E.R. (2003) *The Cognitive Style of Powerpoint*, 2nd edn. Cheshire, CT: Graphics Press LLC.

van Merrienboer, J.J.G., Kirschner, P.A. and Kester, L. (2003) 'Taking the load off a learner's mind: instructional design for complex learning', *Educational Psychologist*, 38 (1): 5–13.

Weissman, J. (2003) *Presenting to Win: The Art of Telling Your Story*, special expanded edn. Upper Saddle River, NJ: FT Prentice Hall.

Wittrock, M.C. (1989) 'Generative processes of comprehension', *Educational Psychologist*, 24 (Fall): 345–76.

Zelazny, G. (2006) *Say It with Presentations*, revised and expanded. edn. New York: McGraw-Hill.

Index

cognitive architecture, 3, 7, 19, 25, 38, 44
auditory channel, 11, 14, 16, 41, 58, 82, 89
dual-channel assumption, 11–12, 17, 26, 29
limitations of, 25, 29, 36, 43, 57, 106
limited capacity assumption, 7–8, 17
long-term memory, 3, 7, 8, 10, 12, 13, 16, 42, 58, 74, 122
schema, 8, 9, 10, 12, 16, 37, 42
sensory memory, 11
visual channel, 11, 14, 16, 26, 41, 58, 89
working memory, 3, 6, 7, 8, 10, 11, 13, 14, 15, 16, 26, 57, 58, 69, 82, 120
cognitive guidance, 27, 28, 35, 36, 43, 74
cognitive information processing (CIP) theory, 9, 10, 11

cognitive load, 3, 13, 14, 15, 16, 24, 25, 26, 28, 43, 48, 69, 76, 84, 89, 107, 120
extraneous, 14, 15, 16, 25, 26, 38, 39
germane, 14, 15, 16, 25, 26, 27, 37
intrinsic, 14, 15, 26
cognitive theory of multimedia learning, 39, 48–9

delivery, 50, 112–26
distracting behaviours, 122
dress, 123
eye contact, 121–2
pacing, 122, 129
questions, 125
rate of speech, 122
signalling, 120–1
slide show controls, 117, 124, 149–50, 179–80
timing, 129
troubleshooting, 118–19

evaluation, 51, 127–9
  formative, 127
  structured self-reflection, 128
  summative, 127–8
  surveys, 128–9

fonts, 85–9, 140
  colour, 88–9
  sans-serif, 85–7
  serif, 85–7
  size, 88
  weight, 88

handouts, 26, 27, 28, 32, 37, 54, 61, 99–107, 117, 119
  advance organizer, 107
  formats, 100, 101–5
  four-page layout, 103–5
  when to use, 106–7

images – see visuals

key points, 35, 36, 38, 57, 58, 61, 62, 76, 78, 82, 119, 122
knowledge, 5, 8, 16, 19, 24, 35, 42
  declarative, 5, 6, 7, 8, 16
  episodic, 5, 28
  prior, 13, 37, 42, 43, 55
  procedural, 5, 6, 7, 8, 16
  semantic, 5, 7, 28

learning, 3, 4, 9, 16, 19, 24, 27, 35, 38, 48, 59
  active processing, 8, 11, 17, 24, 27, 38, 39, 41–2, 57, 69, 107, 121
  assessment of, 128–9
  elaboration, 12, 13, 15, 27, 37, 38, 43, 58, 82, 122
  processing of sounds, 12
  processing of visuals, 12
  recall, 6, 12, 13
  rehearsal, 6, 13
  retention, 4, 16, 37, 38
  transfer, 4, 16, 42
logistics, 49, 53, 54, 59, 120

PowerPoint – see software
preparation:
  instructional analysis, 55–9
  audience analysis, 53, 55–6
  goal analysis, 56–8
  instructional design theory, 47
  rehearsal, 109–13, 120
  script writing, 61–3
  sequence of slides, 71–2
  slide transitions, 148–9, 161–2, 178–9
  slide show format, 117, 150, 163–5, 180
presentation process model, 44, 47–52
principles of multimedia design, 39–41, 67, 69

coherence, 40
individual differences,
    40–1
modality, 40
multimedia, 39, 69
redundancy, 40
spatial contiguity, 39
temporal contiguity, 39

slide designs – *see* slide
    layout themes
slide layout, 70–83, 136–7,
    156, 170–1
    agenda slide, 71, 72,
        74–5, 77
    bibliography, 59, 83
    bullet points, 34
    bumper slide, 72, 77–8,
        82
    captions, 80
    content slides, 71, 72,
        78–82
    ending slide, 72, 82–3
    headlines on slides, 79–80
    key points slide, 72, 76,
        82
    placeholders, 70, 71,
        135–6, 155, 169–70
    question-and-answer slide,
        72, 82
    sentence-style headlines,
        79
    storyboards, 63–7, 78
    themes, 70, 84, 146, 160,

176–7
    title slide, 65, 71, 72–4,
        83
software:
    Apple Keynote, 62, 87,
        117, 153–65
    Impress (OpenOffice/
        StarOffice), 167–81
    PowerPoint, 21, 23, 31,
        41, 53, 54, 62, 63, 65,
        66, 87, 91, 101, 102,
        116, 117, 135–51

visuals, 66, 69, 80–2, 97
    'chartjunk', 95, 96
    charts, 94–6
    clip art, 80, 143
    data–ink ratio, 95
    diagrams, 80, 84, 92–4
    graphs, 80, 94, 95, 106
    images, 80–2, 84, 89–92,
        142, 158, 174–5
        copyright of, 80, 91–2
        credits, 59, 83, 91
        file formats, 91
        resolution, 90–1
        size, 90–1
        sources, 91
    photographs, 75, 80–2
    picture superiority effect,
        67
    statistical displays, 80, 90,
        94–6, 106